NEED TO CREATE LEGAL AWARENESS ON VISUALLY DISABLED IN HUBBALLI-DHARWAD AREA: AN EMPIRICAL STUDY

DR. ANU PRASANNAN

First published in 2020 by
BecomeShakespeare.com

One Point Six Technologies Pvt Ltd,
123, Building J2, Shram Seva Premises,
Wadala Truck Terminus,
Wadala (E), Mumbai - 400037
T:+91 8080226699

ISBN: 978-93-90266-50-0

TABLE OF CONTENTS

CHAPTER 1

INTRODUCTION

International human rights law proceeds on the assumption that each and every human being, more or less, possess identical capacities in various spheres of life. However, this has been proved wrong as far as persons with disabilities are concerned. This even holds more true in the case of visually disabled persons who are entangled by darkness and remain unaware of their legal rights throughout their life. In most countries and most ages, the blind have been considered with a few outstanding exceptions, as objects of charity, of pity, of contempt, even of cruelty. The pain hidden in those who are surrounded with darkness can be felt from the words of Helen Keller. She explains what blindness is.... the feeling of inexistence and emptiness.....

> I felt as if invisible hands were holding me, and I made frantic efforts to free myself. I struggled – not that struggling helped matters, but the spirit of resistance was strong within me; I generally broke down in tears and physical exhaustion........[1]

There are people who are disabled by birth or acquired disability during the life time. Due to such disability, their dependence is more on others. A disabled person is neglected or ill treated and same care and affection is not extended as is given to ordinary persons. In many instances, their basic needs are not attended. They are subjected to unequal treatment by deliberately forgetting that they are also entitled to all rights and safeguards bestowed in the Constitution of India. The persons with disabilities are equally entitled to the mandates of Articles 14, 16 and 21 as their able bodied

---

[1] Helen Keller, *Story of My Life*, Cosimo, Inc., 2009

counterparts. They equally have the right to a decent and honorable living. State and its instrumentalities in turn have duty towards them and must endeavor to protect and preserve their rights.[2] However, the reality is that there is still ill treatment and this ill treatment or neglect has become a universal phenomenon and mandates a need to analyse the problems connected with disability, extent of disability, factors that led to the need for an International Convention on disability and a new legislation on disability in India in order to enable the persons with disabilities to enjoy the rights and opportunities on the same wavelength at par with other citizens.

The disabled persons among other minority groups constitute the largest minority in the world. According to the data provided by World Health Organization (WHO) around 15 per cent of the world's population or estimated 1 billion population live with disabilities. Out of this, around 80% of persons with disabilities live in low-income States which are less equipped to address their needs. As per 2011 Census, there are 2.68 Crore persons with disabilities in India who constitute 2.21% of the total population. Among these 1.50 crore are male and 1.8 crore are female. These include persons with visual, hearing, speech and locomotor disabilities, mental illness, multiple disabilities and other disabilities. The 2011 Census is represented in Table:1

[2] *K. Srinivasa Rao v. APSRTC and Ors.* Writ Petition Nos. 33462 and 34419 of 2013 Decided on 01 June 2017

Table 1: Office of the Registrar General & Census Commissioner, India; GOI

Persons with Disabilities by Type of Disability Census: 2011

Type of Disability	Persons	Male	Female
Total	2,68,10,557	1,49,86,202	1,18,24,355
In seeing	50,32,463	26,38,516	23,93,947
In hearing	50,71,007	26,77,544	23,93,463
In speech	19,98,535	11,22,896	8,75,639
In movement	54,36,604	33,70,374	20,66,230
Mental retardation	15,05,624	8,70,708	6,34,916
Mental illness	7,22,826	4,15,732	3,07,094
Any other	49,27,011	27,27,828	21,99,183
Multiple disability	21,16,487	11,62,604	9,53,883

Source : Primary data

As the population grows, so too does the number of persons with disabilities. WHO estimates that the blind population will double by 2020 due to rise in population and longevity.[3] India has a gigantic blindness problem and the statistics reveals that of the total population, persons with disabilities suffering from 'seeing disability' are more compared to the other types of disabilities. Blindness is classified into (i) congenital: Bupthalmos also known as infantile glaucoma or

---

[3] Ramesh Verma, Pardeep Khanna et., al, The National Programme for Control of Blindness in India, *The Australasian Medical Journal, 2011; 4(1): 1-3. See also www.ncbi.nlm.nih.gov*

hydropthalmos usually of a simple obstruction type affecting both eyes (ii) traumatic caused by blunt injury, penetrating injury or chemical injury (iii) inflammatory (iv) infective[4] (v) neoplastic (vi) vascular (vii) idiopathic[5] (viii) Senile.[6] The factors, viz. war injuries, occupation hazards[7], HIV/AIDS, malnutrition[8], chronic diseases, accidents[9] and environmental

[4]Infective causes may be Corneal ulcer, Viral keratitis

[5]Inflammation of iris and ciliary body leads to congestion of blood vessels and exudation of fibrin rich fluid and inflammatory cells in the tissues.

[6]Cataract is one of the leading causes of reversible blindness in India.

[7]Occupation-related health problems of workers employed in stone quarrying, land mining, leather industry, glasswork, weaving, diamond cutting, hand embroidery etc.; and children employed in the carpet, cracker and match industry, have not received appropriate and sustained attention, as occupation health has not been considered important enough both by the corporate and those responsible to regulate work standards. At the same time, poor farmers and peasants are very vulnerable to disability as they work for long hours exposed to sunlight, dust and smoke. Amputations, muscular diseases and spinal cord injuries are some common hazards associated with agricultural activities. With mechanization of agriculture these incidents are on the increase. However, there is no parallel improvement in the primary health system in the rural areas.

[8]Inadequate shelter, unhygienic living conditions, lack of sanitation and clean drinking water combined with poor access to health facilities breed disability. Common micronutrient deficiencies that affect disability include:

- Vitamin A deficiency: Blindness
- Vitamin B deficiency: Beri-beri, (inflammation or degeneration of the nerves, digestive system and heart), pellagra(central nervous system and gastro-intestinal disorders, skin inflammation) and anaemia
- Vitamin D deficiency :rickets (soft and deformed bones)
- Iodine deficiency – slow growth, learning difficulties, intellectual disabilities, goitre
- Iron deficiency – anaemia, which impedes learning and activity and is a cause of maternal mortality
- Calcium deficiency – osteoporosis (fragile bones)

See ESCAP, *Economic and Social Survey of Asia and the Pacific*, United Nations Publication, Sales No.E.03.II.F.11, 2003.

[9]Improvements in vehicle design and medical facilities, as well as stronger enforcement of traffic regulations concerning the compulsory use of seat belts (car use) and helmets (motorcycle use), and restrictions on alcohol consumption and other intoxicants need to be treated more seriously than it has been. Studies estimate that by 2020, road traffic accidents will be ranked as the third leading cause of disability in the Asian and the Pacific region. Quadriplegia, paraplegia, brain damage and behavioural disorders are some disabilities common among survivors of such accidents.

See National Human Rights Commission, Know your Rights, Rights of Persons with Disabilities, Know Your Rights Series, New Delhi, 2010.

damage, population growth, medical advances that preserve and prolong life, have all contributed to this population growth. At the same time, the age-old disability based discrimination also persists. The linkage between poverty and disability is also well documented.[10] A study by the World Bank estimated that persons with disabilities may account for nearly one out of every five of the world's poorest population. The study reveals the shocking but grim truth that,

> People with disabilities in the developing world are among the poorest of the poor. With disabled people invisible in development initiatives, hundredsof thousands of people who see themselves as potential and willing contributors to family and national economic activity are instead relegated to the margins of society where they are a perceived and considered as actual burden. The result can be devastating, both to the individual and to the economy[11]

The other major and related issues faced by the visually disabled include (i) Education (ii) Skill Development and Employment (iii) Social Security, Health, Rehabilitation and Recreation (iv) Environmental barriers (v) Accessibility. These problems faced by the visually disabled persons are only a glimpse of many and varied that is yet to be unraveled. Above all, they have to be made legally conscious of their available rights.

---

[10]Author says that disability and poverty are inter linked. As per her view,

[N]ot only does disability add to the risk of poverty, but conditions of poverty add to the risk of disability.

See Elwan, Ann (1999), "Poverty and Disability: A Survey of the Literature Social Protection Discussion Paper No.9932, The World Bank Group", [Online: web] Accessed 12 April 2018, URL:http://siteresources.worldbank.org/DISABILITY/Resources/280658-1172608138489/PovertyDisabElwan.pdf

[11]Deborah, Stienstra et. al. (2002), "Base line Assessment: Inclusion and Disability in World Bank Activities, Canadian Centre on Disability Studies", [Online: web] Assessed 12 May 2018 URL:http://www.iddc.org.uk/dis_dev/mainstreaming/incl_dis_wildbank.doc

India has four major legislation relating to disability:

- Mental Health Care Act, 2017; (Mental Health Act,1987 is replaced by the Act of 2017)

- The Rehabilitation Council of India Act, 1992;[12]

- The Rights of Persons with Disabilities Act, 2016; (Persons with Disabilities (Equal Opportunities, Protection of Rights and Full Participation Act, 1995(PWD Act) is replaced by the Act of 2016);

- The National Trust for Welfare of Persons with Autism, Cerebral Palsy, Mental Retardation and Multiple Disabilities Act, 1999.

The PWD Act was a comprehensive legislation, which aroused a lot of hope and expectation among the persons with disabilities. Apart from an assurance of equal opportunities in all walks of life including education and employment, non-discrimination and removal of barriers (both physical and psychological) it sought to ensure certain affirmative action for their full inclusion. However, the way it was being implemented since its enactment left much to be desired; there was a wide gap between rhetoric and reality. The reasons are not far to seek; the Act suffered from structural and procedural lapses. Most important, it lacked teeth and binding force for its implementation in true spirit. The caveat that reforms should only be undertaken within the limits of State's economic capacity also nullified the potential of the Act for change.

The global disability rights movement can be traced since 1970s, this movement has culminated in the adoption of the United Nations Convention on the Rights of Persons with Disabilities (hereafter referred to as the UNCRPD) as also the Optional Protocol thereto on 13 December 2006. The Convention reflects the worldwide process of law reform

---

[12]Rehabilitation Council of India Act was recently amended. See The Rehabilitation Council of India (Amendment) Act, 2000, Act. No. 38 of 2000[4th September, 2000]

in the field of disability.[13] A glimpse on the evolution of the Convention on disability reflects a saddened reality of the oblivious United Nations human rights machinery. However, it would be wrong to say that the UN system as a whole paid no attention. The specialized agencies like International Labour Organisation (ILO), United Nations Educational, Scientific and Cultural Organisation (UNESCO), United Nations International Children's Emergency Fund (UNICEF) and the WHO were in fact very active on the disability issue and indeed participated actively in the drafting of the UNCRPD.[14] The disability issue figured in the general UN system through the UN Commission for Social Development; as distinct from the Commission on Human Rights which itself demonstrates that the issue was framed more as a social policy issue than a human rights issue. Two resolutions of the General Assembly in the 1970s particularly revealed that they provided an early indication of a shift from a 'caring' agenda to a 'rights' agenda in the context of disability.[15] In 1971 the General Assembly passed a resolution entitled Declaration on the Rights of Mentally Retarded Persons[16] and another milestone Resolution in 1975 entitled Declaration on the Rights of Disabled Persons.[17] The year 1981 was declared by the UN as the International Year of Disabled Persons. To follow through, the General Assembly created a World Programme of Action for Persons with Disabilities (WPA) in 1982[18], and in order to facilitate the implementation of WPA, the UN created the UN Decade of Disabled Persons.[19]

[13] The Convention is the first treaty to impact disability rights exclusively and globally.

[14] Gerard Quinn, A Short Guide to the United Nations Convention on the Rights of Persons with Disabilities, 1 *Eur. Y.B. Disability L*,89(2009)

[15] T. Degener and Y Koster-Dreese (ed.), *Human Rights and Disabled Persons*, (Nijhoff, 1995).

[16] UN General Assembly Resolution 2865 (XXVI), 20 December, 1971. This resolution starts by pointing out that that persons with disabilities enjoy a parity of human rights protection with all other persons.

[17] UN General Assembly Resolution 3447 (XXX), 9 December, 1975.

[18] UN General Assembly Resolution 37/52, 3 December, 1982.

[19] The UN General Assembly proclaimed 1983-1992 the United Nations Decade of Disabled Persons.

Although, the implementation of the World Decade was reviewed several times there was no much progress in the way. Some progress was witnessed when Italy and Sweden proposed drafting a new human rights convention on the rights of persons with disabilities. However, due to treaty fatigue, the General Assembly declined to consider a new Convention and instead they opted for a special resolution entitled the UN Standard Rules for the Equalisation of Opportunities for Persons with Disabilities, 1993[20] which was instrumental in moving away from the traditional "welfare approach" towards a "rights-based" approach for more than eight years.[21] The negotiations on the convention originated in an initiative taken by Mexico during the World Conference against Racism, Racial Discrimination, Xenophobia and Related Intolerance held in Durban, South Africa, from 31 August to 7 September 2001.[22] At that conference, Mexico invited the UN General Assembly to adopt an International Convention to protect the rights of persons with disabilities. At the 56th session of the General Assembly in 2001, Mexican President Vincente Fox Quesada reiterated the need for a

[20]Adopted by General Assembly Resolution 48/96, 20 December 1993 .Though comprehensively drafted it lacked legal status in spite of Rule 14 which provided that if they gained sufficient support they might obtain the status of customary international law.

[21]In the 1940s and 1950s the United Nations gave emphasis in promoting the well-being and rights of persons with disabilities through a range of social welfare approaches. The United Nations provided assistance to Governments in disability prevention and the rehabilitation of disabled persons through advisory missions, workshops for the training of technical personnel and the setting up of rehabilitation centres and in 1970s, a shift could be witnessed towards the concept of human rights of persons with disabilities and equalization of opportunities for them.

[22]The UN drafting process began in 2001 and the treaty was adopted in 2006 following eight adhoc sessions of negotiation. The treaty was open for signature in March 2007, ultimately coming into force in May 2008. The drafting process was unique as there was participation by civil society, particularly groups focused on issues of disability or Disabled Peoples Organisations (DPOs) themselves. This was new for the development of any UN treaty as it reflected the needs and desires of persons with disabilities around the world allowing them to live full participatory lives in the society. See Esme Grant and Rhonda Neuhaus, Liberty and Justice for All: The Convention on the Rights of Persons with Disabilities,*19 ILSA J. Int'l and Comp. L. 347 (2013)*

comprehensive and integral convention and presented a proposal for the same which resulted in the establishment of an Ad Hoc Committee.[23] In response to this, the General Assembly by its Resolution 56/168 of 19 December 2001 decided to establish an Ad Hoc Committee to consider the proposal for a Comprehensive and Integral International Convention to Promote and Protect the Rights and Dignity of Persons with Disabilities based on a holistic approach. Thus the Ad Hoc Committee started its negotiations[24] on the draft convention at its third session from 24 May to 4 June 2004 (A/AC/265/2004/5) based on the draft text prepared by the working group in accordance with General Assembly Resolution 58/246. The negotiations went through eight sessions and finalized the negotiations which resulted in the adoption of the International Convention on the Rights of Persons with Disabilities and Optional Protocol. India signed the Convention on the opening day itself and ratified it on 1 October 2007.

Having ratified the Convention, it became imperative for India to harmonise all disability-related legislation and policy provisions in keeping with the guiding spirits and ethos of the Convention. To achieve this objective, the government replaced the Persons with Disabilities (Equal Opportunity Protection of Rights and Full Participation) Act of 1995 with a new legislation, that is, the Rights of Persons with Disabilities Act, 2016 (hereafter referred to as RPWDAct)

---

[23]The General Assembly by its Resolution 56/168 of 19 December 2001 decided to establish an Ad Hoc Committee

[24]One of the unique characteristics within the process of drafting and negotiating the convention has been the active involvement of civil society. Disabled Peoples Organizations (DPOs) and NGOs have established the International Disability Caucus (IDC). This is a consortium of approximately fifty organizations that provided critical input into the convention process, including detailed comments on the draft articles, and making comments on key issues. During the Second Ad Hoc Committee meeting it was agreed that UN accredited NGOs and DPOs could attend any public meetings of the committee and make statements within the plenary sessions, when required See Lang, Raymond (2006), "Human Rights and Disability-New and Dynamic Perspective with the United Nations Convention on Disability", *Asian and Pacific Disability Rehabilitation Journal*, 17(1):3-11.

The 2016 legislation is no doubt an improvement over the 1995 Act which treated disability in only medical parlance. Salient features of the Act can be summed up as follows:

- The Act covers 21 categories of disabilities compared to 7 in the 1995Act[25]

- The persons with disabilities enjoy various rights such as right to equality, life with dignity, respect for his or her integrity, etc., equally with others

- Duties and responsibilities of the appropriate Government have been enumerated

- All educational institutions funded by appropriate Government are to provide inclusive education to the children with disabilities

- National fund is proposed to provide financial support to persons with disabilities

- Stakeholder's participation in the policy making through Central and State Advisory Boards

- Reservation in education and employment sectors

- Increase in reservation in posts from existing 3 per cent to five per cent in the vacancies for persons or class of persons with benchmark disabilities in every establishment and reservation of seats for students with benchmark disabilities in higher educational institutions including persons with blindness and low vision

- Incentives to employees in private sector

- Vocational training and self-employment schemes including loans under concessional rates

- Special schemes and development programmes for persons with benchmark disabilities

- Right to free legal aid and penal provisions for offences committed against them

[25]Nineteen specified disabilities have been defined in the new Act.

- Not to subject persons with disabilities to any medical procedure which leads to infertility without their free and informed consent

- Access to information on reproductive and family planning as their able bodies counterparts.

- Right to access to justice and to any programme, scheme, facility or service offered by National and State Legal Services Authorities under Legal Services Authorities Act, 1987

- Setting up of National and State Commission to act as Grievance Redressal Mechanism, monitor implementation of the proposed legislation replacing the Chief Commissioner and the Sate Commissioners for persons with disabilities

- Guidelines to be issued by the Central Government for issuance of certificates of specified disabilities

- Penalties for offences committed against persons with disabilities; and

- Court of Session to be designated as Special Court by the State Government in every   district to try offences

- Adequate social security measures within the limits of economic capacity of the government.

The PWD Act of 1995 had defined persons with disabilities as those having not less than 40 percent of disability and identified only seven categories of disability such as (i) Blindness (ii)Low vision(iii) Leprosy-cured(iv) Hearing impairment(v) Locomotor disability (vi) Mental retardation(vii)Mental illness. Instead of seven disabilities, the new Act covers 21 conditions and has defined visual impairment under specified disability which includes 'blindness' and 'low vision'. While the 1995 Act had identified only the following seven categories of disability, that is,[26] (i) Blindness, (ii) Low vision, (iii) Locomotor disability, (iv) Leprosy cured, (v) Hearing Impairment, (vi) Mental retardation,[27] (vii) Mental illness and defined 'person with disability' as one suffering from not less than forty per cent of any disability as certified by the medical authority,[28] the RPWD, 2016 has categorised persons with disabilities into three categories: (i) person with disability (ii) person with benchmark disability (iii) person with disability having high support needs. "Persons with disability" is defined as a person with long term physical, mental, intellectual or sensory impairment which hinder his full and effective participation in society equally with others.[29] "Person with benchmark disability" means a person with not less than forty per cent of a specified disability where specified disability has not been defined in measurable terms and includes a person with disability as certified by the

---

[26]Before the PWD Act the following five categories were officially used in India (i) Visually handicapped (ii) speech and hearing handicapped (iii) locomotor handicapped (iv) mentally retarded (v) neurologically handicapped – in this category, the concern is restricted to only the cerebral palsied. See Ali, Baquer and Anjali Sharma (1997), *Disability: Challenges Vs Responses*, New Delhi: Concerned Action Now.

[27]Mental retardation and blindness are defined in the same manner as that in the RCI Act; while in case of hearing impairment it is the loss of sixty decibel or more in the better ear in the conversational range of frequencies, compared to loss of 70 decibel or more under RCI Act

[28]Although a comprehensive legislation, the reality was that it lacked teeth and binding force for its implementation and the caveat that reforms should only be undertaken within the limits of State's economic capacity also nullified the potential of the Act for change. All these led to a need for amendment in the legislation which resulted in108 amendments to the PWD Act including 50 new provisions. However, the Disabled Rights Group (DRG) raised voice for a brand new law on disability. In the midst of these developments, India ratified the UN Convention on the Rights of Persons with Disabilities (UNCRPD) and the need for a new law on disability by harmonizing all related legislations with the ethos of the Convention strengthened. This resulted in the Rights of Persons with Disabilities Bill, 2011. However, Ministry replaced 2011 Bill with 2012 Bill. The Bill of 2012 was not comprehensive and inclusive and there were serious issues raised before the Ministry on the notification of 2012 draft, however, the Cabinet scrutinized and approved it in December, 2013 and finally the 2014 Bill was replaced by the Act of 2016.

[29]The definition provided by the Brand new law on disability in India corresponds the definition of the UN Disability Convention.

certifying authority. Further, the Act also defines "person with disability having high support needs" as a person with benchmark disability certified under clause (a) of sub section (2) of section 58 who needs high support.

Under the category of visual impairment, the Act has defined blindness and low vision as follows:

Blindness: means a condition where a person has any of the following conditions, after best correction —

(i)   total absence of sight; or

(ii) visual acuity less than 3/60 or less than 10/200 (Snellen) in the better eye with best possible correction; or

(iii) limitation of the field of vision subtending an angle of less than 10 degree.

Low-vision: means a condition where a person has any of the following conditions, namely: —

(i)   visual acuity not exceeding 6/18 or less than 20/60 upto 3/60 or upto 10/200 (Snellen) in the better eye with best possible corrections; or

(ii) limitation of the field of vision subtending an angle of less than 40 degree up to 10 degree[30]

The 2016 Act is indeed a much awaited remedy for the disabled community. However, there is great need to sensitize the disabled community of their rights which is the responsibility of every able bodied peer groups. There is more obligation on the government to protect their rights and should be taken care that economic constraints should not come in the way of implementation of their rights.

[30]Clause (zc) of Sec. 2of RPWD Act, 2016

1.1 Objectives:

- To make visually disabled persons legally conscious of their rights under the existing legislative provisions

- To examine critically the policy measures taken by the Government of India with regard to implementation of economic, social and cultural rights as also civil and political rights, and thereby analysing their impact on empowerment of the persons with disabilities.

- To analyse the role of civil society in the implementation process.

- To educate the organizers and instructors working in blind schools in order to achieve the objective of 'inclusive education'

1.2 Research Questions:

- To what extent the visually impaired are aware of their rights?

- Are the social security measures adequate to protect the rights of visually impaired?

- Whether the legislative and administrative measures are adequate in the implementation of the Persons with Disabilities Act, 2016 in India?

- What will be the cost to implement the Act?

- Will there be any economic constraint for implementing the Act?

- What will be the barriers in the implementation of the Act, apart from the economic constraints?

- What is the role of civil society in the implementation of the Act?

1.3 Research Methodology:

The study will be both doctrinal and non doctrinal in nature. Analytical and historical methods will also be followed for carrying out this study. Accordingly, primary and secondary source materials will be utilised extensively for completion of the study. In addition, the official reports and other publications of the United Nations and other global bodies as also various departments/ministries of the State Government will also be used in all possible ways. The empirical study will focus on the visually impaired persons with disabilities in the Hubballi- Dharwad area mainly in schools and rehabilitation centres by using Questionnaire method, Interview, Schedule, case study etc., as research tools for the collection of the proposed data.

1.4 Structure of the study:

The present study will be divided into five chapters. The first chapter, **Introduction** analyses the problems connected with disability, extent of disability, factors that led to the need for a new legislation on disability in India in order to enable the persons with disabilities to enjoy the rights and opportunities on the same wavelength at par with other citizens.

Chapter 2, **Legislative and Administrative Measures** makes an effort to elaborate briefly all major legislation and statutes on disability and also elaborates the role of administrative wherein, an effort will be made to analyze critically the major schemes and programmes launched and implemented by the departments/ministries of the State Government for empowering the visually impaired.

Chapter 3, **Empirical Study on Visually Impaired in Hubballi- Dharwad area** seeks to analyse the extent of legal awareness of the new legislation and to ascertain their views to help them to become part of the society as their able bodied peers and to make suggestions to improve the quality of their lives.

Chapter 4, **Inclusive Educational Measures as a Remedy** aims to integrate the visually impaired with their able bodied peers with a view to harmonise the national legislation on disability in lines with the UN Disability Convention (UNCRPD) and also to analyse its adaptability in Hubballi-Dharward.

The concluding chapter provides an exploratory overview of the need to be taken by the State government in the implementation of the Act and offers certain constructive suggestions for accelerating and streamlining the actualisation of the goal of empowering the visually impaired.

CHAPTER 2

LEGISLATIVE AND ADMINISTRATIVE MEASURES

Disability once viewed as a stigma in the society discriminated persons with disabilities all over the world irrespective of their gender and they continued to suffer from discrimination, lower standards of living and problems of social exclusion. In other words, despite their varied living conditions, the disabled had one thing in common — experience of being exposed to discrimination and exclusion. They were excluded from the mainstream of society and denied their basic human rights. As the response to disability started changing since 1970s there is a growing tendency to view disability as a human rights issue. The shift from the medical model towards viewing disability as a human rights issue has been gradual and well within the legislative and administrative framework. However, it is disheartening that human rights abuses against persons with disabilities, especially in institutional settings, are prevalent even today in several States of the world in one way or the other. This discrimination is more for the visually disabled community and they often tumble upon when they struggle in their journey for gaining education, employment and social integration. This is despite the fact that the Constitution of India applies uniformly to every legal citizen of India, whether they are able or disabled either physically or mentally. Although the Preamble to the Constitution clearly states "…secure to all its citizens; Justice, Social, Economic and Political; Liberty of thought, expression, belief, faith and worship; Equality of status and of opportunity and to promote among them all, Fraternity assuring the dignity of the individual and the unity and integrity of the Nation....",

Indian Constitution is to an extent silent on disability. As the formal recognition of discrimination on the ground of disability is a recent development, it is pertinent in this backdrop to look into all major legislations and statutes on disability and also to elaborate the role of administrative measures in the form of major schemes and programmes launched and implemented by the departments/ministries of the State Government for empowering the visually impaired.

2.1 GLIMPSE OF THE STRUGGLE FOR RECOGNITION OF THE RIGHTS OF PERSONS WITH DISABILITIES

In the struggle for the recognition of their rights, they had to face opposition from all walks which they could overcome because of the support of the Disabled Rights Groups. This calls for a need to look into the Disability Rights Movement (DRM) and as to how they gained strength and momentum in the individual struggle of each disabled persons in the society. Throughout the 1970s and 1980s, the DRM remained largely a battle between few individuals against the system and society. The 1980s saw a shift in the policy framework and 1990s brought drastic changes in the disability sector itself. A distinct self advocacy movement of persons with disabilities which started during the 1970s began campaigning for protection and recognition of their human rights. They advocated the enactment of a comprehensive legislation with a rights based approach and government finally heeded to the demands of DRM recognizing the need for a legislation in 1980. Since the legislative power regarding disability was kept on the State List there was no progress for a long time.[31] However, with the signing of the Proclamation of Equality and Full Participation of People with Disabilities

---

[31]Article 253 of the Constitution of India confers an overriding power on Parliament to make laws for the whole or any part of India for implementing any treaty, agreement or Convention with any other country or countries or any decision made at any international conference, association or other body.

in the Asia and Pacific Region, the Persons with Disabilities Act was enacted by Parliament in 1995.

In order to be included in the census also they had to wait for a long time. The persons with disabilities were indeed excluded from the population census until 1980s as their status was not canvassed in the Indian Census from 1941 to 1971. The 1981 census included information on three types of disabilities. Again, they were totally left out from the purview of the 1991 census which resulted in growing demand by PWD for their inclusion in the population census of India. After a prolonged advocacy, the question on disability was finally included in the 2001 census questionnaire at the last minute. With minimal awareness and training, the enumerators found that 2.1 percent of the total population of the country consists of PWD. India finally accepted that 21 million of its citizens were PWD. However, persons belonging to many more disabilities, including persons with mental and intellectual disabilities, were completely excluded.[33] Evidently, much depended on how disability is defined. The 2011 census however, revealed that over 2.68 crore people in India suffer from some kind of disability. This is equivalent to 2.21 percent of the population. Among the total disabled in the country, 14.9 million are males and 11.8 million are females; 18.6 million PWD reside in rural areas while 8.2 million reside in urban areas.

Looking at this situation and the demands from civil society, the Union Government came up with a National Policy on Disability in the year 2006. This was a comprehensive national policy on disability covering critical areas like education, employment, support services, access, social security, etc. However, this policy was also felt to be

[32]Martand Jha, The history of India's Disability Rights Movement, The *Dipomat*, December 21. 2016

[33]Only five categories of persons with disabilities were included in the census. Disability rights activists strongly dispute the census 2001 figures on the number of persons with disabilities on various grounds: the non-inclusion of many disabilities, the improper training of enumerators in identifying persons with disabilities, etc.

modified in the light of the UN Convention. Somehow, the national policy is nearly silent on the civil and political rights of persons with disabilities. Unfortunately, most of the states of India do not have a state-level disability policy in place. However, a few states are in the process of evolving such a policy. Before analyzing the Karnataka State Policy on disability it is pertinent to look through the disability legislations in India and thereby, the background for the enactment of the comprehensive legislation on disability in India.

2.2 LEGISLATIONS ON DISABIITY IN INDIA

India has four major legislation relating to disability. They are as follows:

- Mental Health Care Act, 2017; (Mental Health Act,1987 is replaced by the Act of 2017)

- The Rehabilitation Council of India Act, 1992;

- The National Trust for Welfare of Persons with Autism, Cerebral Palsy, Mental Retardation and Multiple Disabilities Act, 1999.

- The Rights of Persons with Disabilities Act, 2016; (Persons with Disabilities (Equal Opportunities, Protection of Rights and Full Participation Act, 1995 is replaced by the Act of 2016)[34]

The analysis of the legislations on disability emphasising its salient features with its recent amendments in consonance with the UN Convention on Disability is also given:

- Mental Health Care Act, 2017[35] (No.10 of 2017)

---

[34]Parliament passed the Rights of Persons with Disabilities Bill, 2016 in the winter session of December 2016, which replaced the existing PWD Act which was enacted 21 years back, after making amendments to the 2014 Bill.

[35]Mental Health Care Act 2017 which provides for protection and promotion of rights of persons with mental illness during the delivery of health care in institutions and in community was passed by the Rajya Sabha unanimously on 8th August, 2016

The Mental Health Act, 1987 predates the human rights emphasis in the nineties. It can be described as a civil rights legislation as it aimed to regulate standards in mental health institutions and to make provisions with respect to their property and affairs whereas, the 2017 Act provides for mental healthcare and services for persons with mental illness and to protect their rights during delivery of these mental healthcare and services.[36]

The 1987 Act had defined 'mentally ill person' as one who is in need of treatment by reason of any mental disorder other than mental retardation. However, 2017 Act does not define a mentally ill person but confines to mental illness.[37]

The salient features of the Act are as follows:

(i) The Act aims to safeguard the rights of persons with mental illness along with access to healthcare and treatment without discrimination from the government

(ii) The Act seeks to decriminalize the attempt to commit suicide. The most important feature is that a person attempting suicide shall be presumed to be suffering from severe stress[38] and hence exempted from trial and punishment.

(iii) The Act also imposes a duty on the government to rehabilitate such persons to ensure that there is no recurrence of attempt to suicide.

---

[36]The Act of 1987 had been widely criticized for providing to be inadequate to protect the rights of mentally ill persons.

[37]Under Sec 2 (s) of the Mental Health Care Act 2017, Mental illness means a substantial disorder of thinking, mood, perception, orientation or memory that grossly impairs judgment, behaviour, capacity to recognise reality or ability to meet the ordinary demands of life, mental conditions associated with the abuse of alcohol and drugs, but does not include mental retardation which is a condition of arrested or incomplete development of mind of a person, specially characterised by sub normality of intelligence

[38]The word mental illness in the old act is substituted with 'severe stress.'

(iv) Insurers are bound to make provisions for medical insurance for the treatment of mental illness on the same basis as is available for the treatment of other physical ailments.[39]

(v) The Act has adopted a different approach empowering the individual to make decisions concerning the mental health care or treatment which is in line with the objectives of the UN Convention.[40]

- The Rehabilitation Council of India Act, 1992[41] (No.34 of 1992)

The Rehabilitation Council of India was set up by the Government of India in 1986 initially as a society to regulate and standardize training policies and programmes in the field of rehabilitation of persons with disabilities. The urgent need for minimum standards was felt as the majority of persons engaged in education, vocational training and counselling of persons with disabilities were not professionally qualified. Poor academic and training standards adversely affect the chances of disabled succeeding in the world of work. Therefore, an Act of Parliament in 1992 enhanced the status of the Council to a statutory body with following aims:

1. To standardize training courses for professionals dealing with people with disabilities;

2. To prescribe minimum standards of education and training of various categories of professionals dealing with people with disabilities;

3. To regulate these standards in all training institutions

---

[39]See Section 21(4) of the Act.

[40]The Act seeks to fulfill India's International Obligation pursuant to signing of the Convention.

[41]The Rehabilitation Council of India (RCI) was set up as a registered society in 1986.On September, 1992 the RCI Act was enacted by Parliament and it became a statutory body on 22 June 1993. The Act was amended by Parliament in 2000 to make it broader in its objectives.

uniformly throughout the country;

4. To promote research in rehabilitation and special education; and

5. To maintain Central Rehabilitation Register for registration of professionals.

Coming to the definitional part, the Act has used the term 'handicapped' instead of disability. According to this definition :[42]

'Handicapped' means a person suffering from any disability referred to in clause (i) of Section 2 of the Persons with Disabilities Act, 1995. They are listed as follows:

(i)   blindness;

(ii)   low vision ;[43]

(iii)   leprosy-cured;

(iv)   hearing impairment

(v)   locomotor disability

(vi)   mental retardation

(vii) mental illness

It is to be noted that the in spite of a new comprehensive legislation on disability repealing the Persons with Disabilities Act, 1995 the same definition is continuing as unchanged which calls for a need for amendment of the Rehabilitation Council of India Act to bring it in consonance with the new Act of 2016 and UN Convention on disability.

---

[42]The Rehabilitation Council of India Act, 1992 was amended in the year 2000. The (Amendment) Act, 2000 has amended the definition of handicapped in order to bring it in conformity with clause (i) of Section 2 of the Persons with Disabilities Act, 1995

[43]The 1992 Act defined visually handicapped in a different manner. As per the definition, visually handicapped means a person who suffers from any of the following conditions namely, (i) total absence of sight; or (ii) visual acuity not exceeding 6/60 or 20/200 (snellen) in the better eye with the correcting lenses; or (iii) limitation of the field of vision subtending an angle of degree 20 or worse.

- The National Trust for Welfare of Persons with Autism, Cerebral Palsy, Mental Retardation and Multiple Disabilities Act, 1999 (No.44 of 1999).

As certain groups among the disabled are more vulnerable than others, a special enactment for the protection of such persons, their property and well-being was therefore felt necessary. The enactment of the National Trust for Welfare of Persons with Autism, Cerebral Palsy, Mental Retardation and Multiple Disabilities Act, 1999 (referred to as the National Trust Act) aims to fulfill a common demand of families seeking reliable arrangement for their severely disabled wards. The specific objectives of the Act are:

(i) To enable and empower persons with disabilities to live as independently and as fully as possible within and as close to the community to which they belong;

(ii) To promote measures for the care and protection of persons with disabilities in the event of death of their parent or guardian; and

(iii) To extend support to registered organisations to provide need based services during the period of crisis in the family of disabled covered under this Act.

According to this Act, persons with disability means a person suffering from any of the conditions relating to autism,[44] cerebral palsy,[45] mental retardation,[46] or a combination of any two or more of such conditions and includes a person suffering from severe multiple disability. Ministry

---

[44]Autism means a condition of uneven skill development primarily affecting the communication and social abilities of a person, marked by repetitive and ritualistic behaviour.

[45]Cerebral Palsy means a group of non progressive condition of a person characterized by abnormal motor control posture resulting from brain insult or injuries occurring in the pre natal or infant period of development.

[46]Mental retardation means a condition of arrested or incomplete development of mind of person, which is specially characterized by sub normality of intelligence.

of Social Justice and Empowerment has adopted various schemes for early intervention of persons with disability through therapies, training and providing support to family members,[47] to enhance interpersonal and vocational skills[48],to provide respite homes for orphans or abandoned, families in crisis etc.,[49]

- The Rights of Persons with Disabilities Act, 2016 (No. 49 of 2016)

The PWD (Equal Opportunities, Protection of Rights, and Full Participations) Act, 1995 was enacted to give an effect to the "Proclamation on the Full Participation and Equality of the People with Disabilities in the Asian and Pacific Region." The Proclamation was issued in a meeting of the Economic and Social Commission for Asia and the Pacific Region in December 1992 at Beijing, to launch the "Asian and Pacific Decade of Disabled Persons 1993–2002".[50] The 1995 Act although a comprehensive legislation on disability provided the legal basis for a rights-based inclusive society wherein, the Central and State governments had the right to

---

[47]The scheme is by name DISHA (Early intervention and School Readiness scheme),

[48]VIKAAS Scheme which is a day care scheme

[49]This is by name SAMARTH that aims at setting up Samarth Centres for providing group home facility for all age groups with adequate and quality care service with acceptable living standards including provision of basic medical care. The other schemes include GHARAUNDA (Group Home for Adults), NIRAMAYA (Health Insurance Scheme), SAHYOGI(Caregiver training Scheme), GYAN PRABHA 9Educational Support), PRERNA (Marketing Assistance), SAMBHAV (Aids and Assisted Devices), BADHTE KADAM (Awareness and community interaction) etc.

[50]The Governments of 58 per cent of the world's population made a historic decision in the concluding year of the United Nations Decade of Disabled Persons (1983-1992). The Economic and Social Commission for Asia and the Pacific (ESCAP), at its forty-eighth session in April 1992, declared the period 1993 to 2002 as the Asian and Pacific Decade of Disabled Persons. The unique regional initiative was launched at a meeting convened by ESCAP at Beijing in December 1992. That meeting adopted the Proclamation on the Full Participation and Equality of People with Disabilities in the Asian and Pacific Region, and the Agenda for Action for the Asian and Pacific Decade of Disabled Persons. The Proclamation and Agenda for Action for the Decade were endorsed by the Commission at its forty-ninth session in April 1993.

play the lead role in making the rights actionable.[51] The Act adopted an approach of social welfare in respect of PWD and the main focus was on prevention and early detection of disabilities, education and employment of the PWD. The Act also provided 3% reservation in Government jobs and educational institutions. It stressed on making the barrier-free situations as a measure of nondiscrimination. The inherent gaps, lacunas and defects in the Act necessitated a need for amendment in the legislation which resulted in108 amendments to the PWD Act including 50 new provisions. However, the DRG raised voice for a brand new law on disability. In the midst of these developments, India ratified the UNCRPD and the need for a new law on disability by harmonizing all related legislations with the ethos of the Convention strengthened. This resulted in the Rights of Persons with Disabilities Bill, 2011. However, Ministry replaced 2011 Bill with 2012 Bill. The Bill of 2012 was not comprehensive and inclusive and there were serious issues raised before the Ministry on the notification of 2012 draft, however, the Cabinet scrutinized and approved it in December, 2013 and finally the 2014 Bill was replaced by the Act of 2016.

The Principles stated to be implemented for empowerment of persons with disabilities through the Rights of Persons with Disabilities Act, 2016 are respect for inherent dignity, individual autonomy including the freedom to make one's own choices, and independence of persons. The Act lays stress on non-discrimination, full and effective participation and inclusion in society, respect for difference and acceptance of disabilities as part of human diversity and humanity, equality of opportunity, accessibility, equality between men and women, respect for the evolving capacities of children with disabilities, and respect for the right of children with

---

[51]For more details see Annual Report 2004-2005 of National Human Rights Commission (NHRC), New Delhi.

disabilities to preserve their identities. The principle reflects a paradigm shift in thinking about disability from a social welfare concern to a human rights issue. In this context an attempt is made to look into the schemes and programmes of the governments both at the Centre and State and thereafter, administrative measures in the implementation of the rights of the persons with disabilities in the Central and the State Government of Karnataka.

2.3 Central and State Government Schemes and Programmes

Although the subject of disability figures in the State List in the Seventh Schedule of the Constitution, the Government of India under the Ministry of Social Justice and Empowerment (MSJE) has always been proactive in the disability sector. The Government of India formulated the National Policy for Persons with Disabilities (NPPD) in February 2006[52] which deals with Physical, Educational and Economic Rehabilitation of persons with disabilities. In addition, the policy also focuses upon rehabilitation of women and children with disabilities, barrier free environment, social security; research etc., The focus of the policy is on the following:

- Prevention of Disabilities

- Rehabilitation Measures

- Women and children with disabilities

- Barrier free environment

- Issue of Disability Certificates

- Social Security

- Promotion of Non- Governmental Organisations

---

[52]The National Policy recognizes the fact that a majority of persons with disabilities can lead a better quality life if they have equal opportunities and effective access to rehabilitation measures.

- Collection of regular information on persons with disabilities

- Research

- Sports, Recreation and cultural life

The MSJE is the nodal Ministry to coordinate all matters relating to the implementation of the Policy. Every five years a comprehensive review will be done on the implementation of the National Policy. A document indicating status of implementation and a roadmap for five years shall be prepared based on the deliberations in a national level convention. Based on this, State Governments and Union Territory administrations will be urged to take steps for drawing up State Policy and develop action plan.

MSJE is not only running seven National Institutes (NIs) dealing with various types on disabilities and seven Composite Regional Centers (CRCs) which provide rehabilitation services to Persons with disabilities but also runs courses for rehabilitation professionals.[53] Funds are also provided to large number of NGOs for similar services. National Handicapped Finance and Development Corporation (NHFDC), a non-profit company under MSJE provides loans at concessional interest rates to persons with disabilities for self-employment.

---

[53]The seven National Institutes (NIs) are (i) Ali Yavar Jung National Institute for Hearing Handicapped (AYJNIHH), (ii) National Institute for Empowerment of Persons with Multiple Disabilities (NIEPMD) Chennai, (iii)Swami Vivekanand National Institute of Rehabilitation (SVNIRTAR) Cuttack, (iv) National Institute for Orthopedically Handicapped (NIOH) Kolkata, (v) National Institute of Visually Handicapped (NIVH),(vi) National Institute of Mentally Handicapped (NIMH) Secundrabad, and (vii) Pandit Deen Dayal Upadhyaya Institute for Physically Handicapped (IPH) New Delhi. To overcome the lack of adequate facilities for rehabilitation of Persons with Disabilities, the Ministry of Social Justice and Empowerment has set up seven Composite Regional Centres for Persons with Disabilities at Srinagar (JandK), Sundernagar (Himachal Pradesh), Lucknow (U.P.), Bhopal (M.P.), Guwahati (Assam), Patna (Bihar), Ahmedabad (Gujarat) and Kozhikode (Kerala) to provide both preventive and promotional aspects of rehabilitation like education, health, employment and vocational training, research and manpower development, rehabilitation for persons with disabilities etc.

In the 11th Five Year Plan it was stated that 'The 'Disability Division' of the MSJE will be strengthened by converting it into a separate department so that it can liaise effectively with all the other concerned Ministries/Departments and fulfill its responsibilities towards the disabled. To further the decision, as of now two departments have been created under the MSJE vide notification dated 12.5.2012, viz:-

(i) Department of Social Justice and Empowerment (Samajik Nyaya and Adhikarita Vibhag)

(ii) Department of Disability Affairs (Nishaktata Karya Vibhag)[54]

In what can be termed as a big step forward for the Indian disability sector, the Department of Empowerment of Persons with Disabilities was carved out of MSJE as department of disability affairs to ensure greater focus on policy matters to effectively address disability issues and to act as nodal department for greater co-ordination among stakeholders, organizations, State Governments and related Central Ministries. The department has been renamed as DIVYANGJAN. MSJE has adopted various schemes and programmes for the persons with disabilities. The disability certificate is the basic document that a person with any disability of more than 40% requires in order to avail any facilities, benefits or concessions under the available schemes.[55] Some of the initiatives by the Central and State Government are listed below:

- Assistance for purchase/fitting of aids and appliances (ADIP Scheme)

- Scheme for Implementation of Rights of Persons with Disabilities Act, 2016 (SIPDA)

---

[54]It is renamed as Department of Empowerment of Persons with Disabilities

[55]The disability certificate has to be issued by a Medical Board in keeping with the guidelines for evaluation of various disabilities and procedure for certification approved by the Centre.

- Deendayal Disabled Rehabilitation Scheme[56] (DDRS Scheme)
- Inclusive Education for the Disabled at Secondary Stage (IEDSS)
- Information Communication and Technology (ICT)
- Technology Development Projects in Mission Mode
- National Awards for Persons with Disabilities
- Vocational Rehabilitation Centers
- Incentives to Private Sector Employers for providing employment to persons with disabilities
- National Scholarship for Persons with Disabilities
- National Programme for the Control of Blindness (NPCB)
- Accessible India Campaign
- Awareness generation and publicity
- ADIP Scheme[57]

Analyzing the schemes and programmes provided under the Central Government, ADIP scheme is to assist the needy disabled person in procuring durable, sophisticated and scientifically manufactured, modern, standard aids and appliances to promote physical, social, psychological rehabilitation of persons with disabilities by reducing the effects of disabilities and at the same time enhance their economic potential. Assistive devices are given to improve their independent functioning. For the visually disabled, assistance is given under six main heads by providing category-wise kits.[58] They are:

[56]Government will implement this scheme through e-Anudaan Portal www.ngograntsje.gov.in

[57]Under ADIP scheme grants in aids of Rs. 430.98 crores have been utilized during last three years (2014-2017) benefiting 7.03 lakh PWDs through 5265 camps across India.

[58]To receive the aid and appliances a bonafide certificate is to be produced along with other documents to ensure the beneficiaries current academic status.

(i)   Kit-1: For primary school children from class 1st to 5th

(ii) Kit-2: For upper primary school children from class 6th to 8th

(iii) Kit-3: For Senior Secondary School Children for 9th and 10th class

(iv) Kit:4: For Higher Secondary and above school children for class 11th and 12th

(v)   Kit: 5: For college students who are blind students and low vision students

(vi) Kit: 6: ADL Kit for adults.

The scheme is implemented through various implementing agencies and the procedure for sanction of grant is as follows:

Procedure for sanction of grant/assistance

Department of Empowerment of Persons with Disabilities

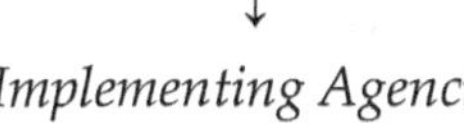

↓

Implementing Agencies

↓

Beneficiary

- Scheme for Implementation of Rights of Persons with Disabilities Act, 2016 (SIPDA)

SIPDA is a central sector scheme approved for continuation during the 14th Finance Commission, that is, up to 2019-20. The scheme covers wide range under which financial assistance is given for undertaking various activates outlined in the Act. The RPWD Act, 2016 endorses the rights of persons with disabilities for access to education, vocational training, employment, public transport, built environment, information and communication and upholds their independence and dignity. The Ministry has been releasing funds under the Scheme since 1999 after the implementation of the provisions of the Persons with Disabilities (Equal

Opportunities, Protection of Rights and Full Participation) Act, 1995. All components of DDRCs will be funded under the SIPDA Scheme only. Four other independent Schemes of the Department viz. Awareness Generation Scheme, Research & Development, In-service Training and Incentives to Employees, have also been merged with the SIPDA Scheme.

Implementing Agencies

(Funds will be released to implementing institutions directly)

    (i)   Department of the State Governments

    (ii) Autonomous Bodies/Statutory Bodies/Public Sector Undertakings by Central, State Govts. etc.,

    (iii) National Institutes/ CRCs/DDRCs/RCs/Outreach Centers under MSJ&E

    (iv) Organisations registered under Societies Registration Act, 1860 or Indian Trusts Act,1882 or Companies Act

    (v) Central/State recognized Sports bodies and Federations

    • DDRS Scheme

Deendayal Disabled Rehabilitation Scheme aims at financial inclusion of persons with disabilities. Under the revised scheme of 2018-19 government provides financial assistance to voluntary organizations for running (i) special schools for persons with intellectual, hearing, speech and visual disabilities, (ii) pre-school and early intervention and training, (iii) projects for children suffering from cerebral palsy, (iv) rehabilitation of leprosy cured persons, (v) community based rehabilitation programmes, (vi) low vision centres, (vii) human resource development etc. The model projects supported under the scheme for the visually disabled include:

- Project for pre-school and early intervention and training

The main objective is to prepare infants and children up

to 6 years of age for schooling in special schools and/or integration at the appropriate stage in regular schools. The project also provides for therapeutic services, day care and counseling of parents.

- Special schools

Special school projects for the mentally challenged, the hearing and speech impaired and the visually challenged are supported under the scheme. The main thrust of special education is to develop communication skills and other sensory abilities with the end objective varying from acquiring daily living skills to integration in regular institutions of learning and society in general. For the visually disabled, special schools aim at providing communication skills and development of other sensory abilities with the end objective being to integrate them in regular institutions of learning and society in general. The objectives provided under the scheme are:

i.   To impart special training on communication and language skills through use of braille script.

ii.   To improve the mobility skills of the visually impaired and facilitate in the use of necessary aids and appliances.

iii.   To give special inputs on managing the daily living skills.

iv.   To tone the other functional senses through special instruction on multi-sensory training.

v.   To provide for special orientation education with reference to the physical, psychological and social environment.

vi.   To cope with the normal literacy levels to prepare and provide opportunities for educational integration that would eventually lead to social integration.

vii. To involve the parents and encourage them in a participative role in the educational process of their child.

viii. To prepare the students for integration in regular schools as far as possible.

ix. To provide support services for visually impaired children studying in integrated/inclusive schools.

The existing norms for the teacher-pupil ratio is kept ranging from 1:15 (normal) to 1:8. The extent of funding will however, be contingent on various factors like availability of resources with the government, the financial capacity of the NGO, delivery of services and activity level of the NGO, the need and justification put forth by the organization, etc. A higher ratio than 1:15 will be considered in deserving cases and in the case of primary schools. Provision is also there for periodical medical and eye check up of students so as to ensure that such of the beneficiaries whose vision can be restored are helped. The services of Ophthalmologist/ Optometrist trained in low vision management can be availed on per visit basis and the visit can be once in 3 months or 6 months depending upon the need.

- Project for low vision centres

These projects provide facilities for medico-rehabilitation of persons with low vision. The centres provide identification, assessment, rehabilitation and counseling services and assist individuals with low vision to reach their maximum potential through guidance and improvement of visual efficiency.

Although the scheme is revised inconsonance with the UNCRPD it has not been revised as per the RPWD Act. The implementation of the scheme is as follows:

Procedure for implementation

Nodal Department in State Government/UT Administration

↓

District Level

↓

Local Level

- Inclusive Education for the Disabled at Secondary Stage (IEDSS)[59]

This scheme supports children with disabilities aged 14 or above for completing their secondary education from class 9 to class 12 in government, local body and government aided schools. The scheme provides for identification of children with disabilities moving from elementary school to secondary and providing them with aids and appliances for their disabilities, access to learning material, transport facilities, hostel facilities, scholarships, books, assistive technologies and provision of scribes and readers. The scheme covers children with blindness, low vision, leprosy cured, hearing impairment, locomotor disabilities, mental retardation, mental illness, autism, and cerebral palsy and may eventually cover speech impairment, learning disabilities, etc. Girls with disabilities receive special focus which will help them to gain access to secondary schools and also to information and guidance for developing their potential. The students with disabilities also get various scholarships to complete higher education. Setting up of Model inclusive schools in every State is envisaged under the scheme. This inclusive education

---

[59]The Scheme of Inclusive Education for Disabled at Secondary Stage (IEDSS) has been launched from the year 2009-10. This Scheme replaces the earlier scheme of Integrated Education for Disabled Children (IEDC). This scheme is now subsumed under Rashtriya Madhyamik Shiksha Abhiyan (RMSA) from 2013. The States/UTs are also in the process of subsuming under RMSA as RMSA subsumed Scheme. For more information see Department of School Education & Literacy under Ministry of Human Resource and Development.

helps them to participate with other non disabled people and paves the way for inclusion.

Implementing Agency

The School Education Department of the State Government/ UT

↓

Beneficiaries

- Information Communication and Technology (ICT)

A mobile app will be launched to provide information on disabled friendly public utilities in a city.[60] New devises are constantly developed in this field such as speech recognition programs for the computer. It will feature places like ATM, banks, malls, toilets and will also have user-generated ratings of how disabled friendly those places are. Government is also planning to introduce set top boxes to make TV programmes more useful for persons with visual impairment.[61] Content on government web-site will also be converted from text to speech mode through screen reader programmes for visually impaired.[62]

Focus of Accessible India Campaign (AIC)

Department of Disability Affairs launched the AIC under Sugamya Bharat Abhiyan

↓

---

[60]Mobile communication also provides people with disabilities with many new possibilities

[61]Currently there is only one news bulletin with sign language for hearing impaired. The government will be training 200 persons in sign language every year for next five years. Sign languages will be introduced in more than 25 per cent of the programmes starting with Dooradarshan to make television more disabled-friendly.

[62]Sandhya Limaye, "Social Empowerment for differently abled", *Yojana*, August 2018

Focus is on

(i) Physical infrastructure (ii) transportation (iii) information & communication technology

- Technology Development Projects in Mission Mode

The scheme which was started during 1990-91, identifies R&D projects and provides funds for developing aids and appliances. The scheme is implemented through the IITs Educational Institutes, Research Agencies and Voluntary Organisations etc. Financial Assistance is provided on 100% basis. The four technical advisory groups monitor the selection of the projects and also their progress at different stages in areas of disabilities including visual impairedness.

Objectives of scheme

Government of India launched Science & Technology Project in Mission Mode on

Application of technology for the welfare & rehabilitation of the handicapped

To coordinate, fund and direct application of technology in utilization of

(i) Suitable and cost effective aids and appliances

(ii) Methods of education and skill development to enhance

(a) Employment (b) easier living and mobility (c) communication (d) recreation   (e) integration in society

- National Awards for People with Disabilities

Every year on the occasion of the International day for the disabled persons[63] the department confers national awards on individuals, institutions, districts etc for outstanding work done by them in the field of empowerment of persons with disabilities. National awards are given under 14 (fourteen) different categories like (i) Best employee/ Self employed with disabilities (ii) Best employers and placement officer or agency (iii) Best individual and institution working for the cause of persons with disabilities (iv) Role model awards (v) Best applied research or innovation or Product development aimed at improving the life of persons with disabilities (vi) Outstanding work in the creation of barrier-free environment for the persons with disabilities (vii) Award for the best district in providing rehabilitation service (viii) Best state channelizing agency of National Handicapped Finance and Development Corporation. (ix) Award for the outstanding creative adult persons with disabilities (x) Award for the best creative child with disabilities (xi) Best braille press (xii) Best accessible website (xiii) Best state in promoting empowerment of persons with disabilities (xiv) Best sports person with disability.

Procedure for sanction of grant/assistance

Advertisement through Directorate of Advertising and Visual Publicity (DAVP)

↓

Screening Committees

↓

National Selection Committee

---

[63]3rd December is celebrated as the International Day for the Disabled Persons.

- Vocational Rehabilitation Centers

The initiative of setting District Disability Rehabilitation Centers (DDRC) was made during ninth five year plan with the active support of State governments. They are provided with financial, infrastructural, administrative and technical support by the Central and State governments so that they are in a position to provide rehabilitation services to persons with disabilities in the concerned districts. Their main objectives are

(i) Survey and identification of persons with disabilities through camp approach

(ii) Awareness generation for encouraging and enhancing prevention of disabilities

(iii) Early intervention

(iv) Therapeutic Services e.g. physio-therapy, occupation therapy, speech therapy etc

(v) Facilitation of issue of disability certificates, bus passes and other concessions and facilities for persons with disabilities

(vi) Referral and arrangements for surgical correction through government and charitable institutes

(vii) Arrangement of loans for self-employment from banks and other financial institutions including State Channelizing Agencies (SCAs) of NHFDC

(viii) Counseling of disabled, their parents and family members

(ix) Promotion of barrier free environment

(x) Provision of supportive and complementary services for promoting education, vocational training and employment of persons with disabilities through:

- Imparting orientation training to teachers, community and families

- Training to persons with disabilities for early motivation and early stimulation for education, vocational training and employment

- Identifying suitable vocations for persons with disabilities keeping in view local resources and designing and providing vocational training and identifying suitable jobs so as to make them economically independent and

- Providing referral services for existing educational, training and vocational institutions

Procedure for Funding

Joint venture of Central and State Governments funded through

↓

Schemes for implementation of the PWD Act 1995 for 3 years

↓

Afterwards through Scheme of Deendayal Disabled Rehablitation Scheme (DDRS)

- Incentives to Private Sector Employers for providing employment to persons with disabilities

The objective of the scheme is to encourage employment of persons with disabilities in the corporate sector. The scheme of giving incentives to employers for providing employment to persons with disabilities in the private sector was launched in the year 2008-09. Under the scheme, payment of employer's contribution towards the Employees Provident Fund Organization (EPFO) and the Employees State Insurance Corporation (ESIC) for the first three years is made by the Government of India in respect of persons with disability appointed in the private sector to a post carrying monthly emoluments up to Rs.25,000/-. The administrative charges of 1.1% of the wages of the employees covered under the Employees Provident Fund and Miscellaneous Provisions (EPF and MP) Act will continue to be paid by the employer.

Procedure for implementation

Department of Empowerment of Persons with Disabilities
(DEPwD)

↓

Employees Provident Fund Organisation (EPFO) and
Employees State Insurance Corporation (ESIC)

↓

Beneficiary

- National Scholarship for persons with disabilities

Scholarship schemes are provided for giving financial assistance to students with disabilities in pre-matric level, IX and X; Post-matric level, XI and XII; and up to Post-graduate degrees/diploma level. In addition, National Overseas Scholarship for students with disabilities are provided for pursuing studies abroad at the level of master's degree and PhD.

Mode of disbursal of scholarship

Department of Empowerment of Persons with Disabilities
(DEPwD)

↓

Beneficiary's Account through PFMS System

- National Programme for the Control of Blindness (NPCB)

NPCB was launched in the year 1976 as a 100 per cent centrally sponsored scheme with the goal to reduce the prevalence of blindness from 1.4% to 0.3%. As per survey in 2001-02, prevalence of blindness is estimated to be 1.1%. Survey on avoidable blindness conducted under NPCB during 2006-07 showed reduction in the prevalence of blindness from 1.1% (2001-02) to 1% (2006-07). Various activities undertaken during the Five Year Plans under NPCB are targeted towards achieving the goal of reducing the prevalence of blindness to 0.3% by the year 2020. The objectives of NPCB in the XII Plan are as follows:

- To reduce the backlog of blindness through identification and treatment of blind at primary, secondary and tertiary levels based on assessment of the overall burden of visual impairment in the country

- Strengthening the existing and developing additional human resources and infrastructure facilities for providing high quality comprehensive eye care in all districts of the country.

- To improve quality of service delivery to the affected population

- To enhance community awareness on eye care and lay stress on preventive measures

- Increase and expand research for prevention of blindness and visual impairment

- To secure participation of voluntary organisations/ private practitioners in eye care.

- To provide best treatment for curable blindness available in the district region

- To set up mechanism for referral coordination and feed-back between organisations dedicated to prevention, treatment and rehabilitation.

Mode of release of funds

Government of India (GOI)

↓

State Blindness Control Society or State Health and Family Welfare Society

(Based on Annual Plan submitted)

* Accessible India Campaign

Department of Empowerment of Persons with Disabilities (DEPwD), Ministry of Social Justice & Empowerment has conceptualized the "Accessible India Campaign (Sugamya Bharat Abhiyan)"as a nation-wide flagship campaign for achieving universal accessibility that will enable persons with disabilities to gain access for equal opportunity and live independently and participate fully in all aspects of life in an inclusive society. The campaign targets at enhancing the accessibility of built environment, transport system and information & communication eco-system.[64] This campaign was launched for creating universal accessibility for persons with disabilities in built environment, transport, information and communication technology (ICT) ecosystem. In this connection a team of experts are working extensively to conduct awareness programmes and workshops for sensitizing all the main stakeholders including builders and activists.

* Awareness generation and publicity

The scheme was launched in 2014 with the objective of

[64]http://disabilityaffairs.gov.in/content/accessible_india.php

providing wide publicity including event based publicity etc through electronic, print, film media, multi media to the schemes and programmes run by the Central and State Governments for the welfare of persons with disabilities. The scheme aims at creating an enabling environment for social inclusion of the persons with disabilities, to disseminate information about the legal rights of the persons with disabilities, to sensitise the employers and other similar groups on the special needs of the specially abled persons, to develop content for rehabilitation of different types of disabilities, provide help line etc.,

Release of fund

After approval of committee consisting

↓

(i) Joint Secretary (Awareness Generation & publicity)

(ii)   representative of IFD (iii)representative of DAVP (iv) special invitee from PWDs (v) director

↓

Disbursements will be with the concurrence of IFD

2.4 Karnataka State Policy and Government Schemes on Disability

Karnataka Govt. passed the Karnataka State policy on Disability on January 9, 2007 which is on the basis of the objectives enshrined in the PWD Act 1995.[65] It has been evolved to create synergy amongst all stake holders, departments and agencies in implementing the provisions of Act in its letter and spirit.

---

[65]Karnataka is one of the model states which have passed a state policy of disabilities.

The Women and Child Development Department[66] is the nodal department and the office of Commissioner for Persons with Disabilities[67] coordinate and monitor the programmes and schemes for persons with disabilities and take steps to safeguard the rights of persons with disabilities. The objectives of the policy are as follows :[68]

- To ensure implementation of the legislations related to persons with disabilities.

- Multi-sectoral coordination amongst concerned agencies for prevention and early detection of disabilities.

- Promotion of education as well as enrolment of children with disabilities in mainstream schools and to formulate a comprehensive education scheme as enshrined in the Disabilities Act.

- Promotion of self-employment amongst persons with disabilities with special focus on Govt. agencies which create opportunities for disabled entrepreneurs to provide services within the various Government agencies and departments.

- Effective implementation of various departmental schemes to promote the development of persons with disabilities.

- Ensure non-discrimination and monitoring of rehabilitation schemes (schemes under the State Government and the Govt. of India)

- Ensure qualitative services to be provided by the voluntary sectors in the field of disabilities.

[66]The department of women and child development under Karnataka state government has been assigned the responsibility to implement various social welfare schemes

[67]The office of the State Commissioner for Persons with Disabilities in Karnataka is established as per chapter XII Sec 60 (1) of the PWD Act, 1995

[68]Available at www.karnataka.gov.in/welfareofdisabled/Pages/Karnataka-State-Policy.aspx

Through the State policy on disability and welfare schemes, the State government aims to safeguard the rights of people with disabilities. The main objectives of the Karnataka government welfare programmes for the disabled people are:

- To ensure rehabilitation

- To provide education and economic opportunities

- To promote self employment

- To ensure non discrimination

The schemes provided by the State Government are as per the Central Government Schemes under the provisions of the PWD Act of 1995.[69] The hierarchy of the Karnataka State Government for the implementation of the rights of persons with disabilities under the Act of 2016 was framed on 13th March, 2018 which is as follows:

State Commissioner

↓

State Advisory Board

↓

District-level Committee (which includes all the departments under sec. 66 of the RPWD Act, 2016)

2.5 Implementation of the Rights of Persons with Disabilities Act in Karnataka

The enactment of the RPWD Act and subsequent notification of the Rights of Persons with Disabilities Rules, 2017 is intended to bring Indian legislation in line with the

---

[69]Apart from the Central Government Schemes, the State Government has also framed its own schemes for the persons with disabilities.

United Nations Convention on the Rights of Persons with Disabilities. The Act provides broad based Central and State Advisory Boards on Disability which are to be set up to serve as apex policy making bodies at the Central and State level. Office of Chief Commissioner of Persons with Disabilities has been strengthened who will now be assisted by 2 Commissioners and an Advisory Committee comprising of not more than 11 members drawn from experts in various disabilities. Similarly, the office of State Commissioners of Disabilities has been strengthened who will be assisted by an Advisory Committee comprising of not more than 5 members drawn from experts in various disabilities. The Chief Commissioner for Persons with Disabilities and the State Commissioners will act as regulatory bodies and Grievance Redressal Agencies and also monitor implementation of the Act. District level committees will be constituted by the State Governments to address local concerns of persons with disabilities. Details of their constitution and the functions of such committees would be prescribed by the State Governments in the rules. The Act enables the appropriate government to designate persons having requisite qualifications and experience as certifying authorities who shall be competent to issue the certificate of disability.[70] National and State Fund will be created to provide financial support to the persons with disabilities. The existing National Fund for Persons with Disabilities and the Trust Fund for Empowerment of Persons with Disabilities will be subsumed with the National Fund. The Act also provides for penalties for offences committed against persons with disabilities and also violation of the provisions of the new law. For studying the implementation of the Rights of Persons with Disabilities Act, 2016 in the State of Karnataka it becomes necessary to analyse the total population in Karnataka.

---

[70]Under section 57(1) of the 2016 Act

2.5.1 Statistics of the State of Karnataka as per 2011 Census

Among the total population of 67.6 million in the State of Karnataka[71] the persons with disabilities as per the 2011 Census is shown in the Table: 2

Table: 2: Government of Karnataka, Handbook of Karnataka Schemes,2016

Sl.No	Types of Disability	Total Population of Persons With Disabilities
1	In Seeing	264170
2	In Hearing	235691
3	In Speech	90741
4	In Movement	271982
5	Mental Retardation	93974
6	Mental Illness	20913
7	Any Other	246721
8	Multiple Disability	100013
	Total	**13,24,205**

Source : Primary data

In the State of Karnataka the office of State Commissioner is at Bangalore with the following staff: (i) State Commissioner

---

[71]As of 2018 there are 68,236,674 people in the State of Karnataka and the 2011 census estimated the population of the State to be 61,130,704.

(ii) Assistant Commissioner and (iii) other six staffs to assist the Bangalore office. Karnataka State Commissioner is appointed as per section 79(1) of the RPWD Act of 2016.[72] Interview with the State Commissioner for PWD enumerated the ongoing stages of the implementation of the RPWD Act of 2016. The provisions of the Act are still under discussion with the different governmental departments of the State along with the non-governmental organizations for the disabled. Each provisions of the Act are looked into by different specific departmental guidelines and specialized non-governmental organizations to draw a concluding scheme for the disabled in the State. The State Government has earlier implemented several of its schemes along with the non-governmental organizations and is still continuing to enhance the same through the enactment of the new Act of 2016.

Fig. 1: State Commissioner Office, Bengaluru

The State Commissioner is of the view that the new Act needs more time and resources for its effective implementation

---

[72]Presently Mr. V. S. Basavaraju is the Karnataka State Commissioner for the Persons with disabilities and the information provided by him is collected based on interview held on 27th August, 2018.

as the Act has categorized 21 disabilities compared to the 7 categories of disabilities as per the earlier enactment. The financial constraints regarding the implementation process touching upon areas of sufficient infrastructure and need for classifying the Central and State facilities and benefits provided as per the schemes and policies by them respectively were highlighted by the State Commissioner.

In the views of the Commissioner, grant provided by State Government to non-government organizations are not sufficient and matching with the total population of disabled but at the same time one Crore rupees has been sanctioned by the State government for the higher education such as for education abroad, for PhD programmes, and other competitive exams. State Government has assisted in paying of Provident Fund to both the employee and employer up to three years of employment. Almost 95 per cent of the majority of disabled population is getting disability pension. A scheme has been made to provide either employment or disability pension under certain employability criteria for types of disabilities including visually impaired. Every year new schemes are implemented in the State and prior to its implementation around five crore rupees is allocated for conducting surveys in the overall categories of disability. In future, the State government may conduct research programmes in every category of disability including the visually impaired and for the implementation of the RPWD Act of 2016 and also survey for the State Government schemes and programmes.

The State Government schemes and programmes are yet to be framed and is ongoing. As per the Central Government schemes and programmes which are to be implemented in the State in parallel collaboration with the State Government is facilitated as per the disabled population and State budget allocation. The State Advisory Board has been recently constituted by the State for State-level consultative and advisory aspects on disability matters as per section 66(1) and 71(1) of RPWD Act of 2016. District-level Committee is yet to be formed as per Section 72 of the RPWD Act, 2016.

Regarding Inclusive Education under the newly enacted Act of 2016 the State Government is compiling its Sarva Sikshana Abiyana, Madyamika Shikshana and other educational programmes into single programme and they are in favour of integrating visually impaired children into the main stream schools.

Insurance schemes for disabled employees are yet to be adopted and are still in its early stage for the benefit of the visually impaired along with other disabilities as per the new enactment.

State has experimented some devices and technologies[73] for traffic controls for visually disabled in some small towns but not yet successfully facilitated throughout the state.

In the area of sports for persons with disabilities including visually impaired, the State government is following a programme under the name "Sadhane" for providing financial assistance to differently abled participating in national and international level games.[74] They are awarded in the State with prize money for winning in the international, national, district and local level sports in the category of

---

[73]With the advancement of science and technology there are advanced devices like Dot which is the world's first Braille smart watch; Braille e-book reader that enables blind and partially sighted people to read easily; Tactile Wand Electronic Stick that helps visually impaired to detect the object that comes in their way; Finger Reader, a wearable tool to help read text with two functions (i) to help the visually impaired read printed text on a book or on an electronic device and also to be used (ii) as a language translation tool etc. But unfortunately these advancements have never reached the visually disabled community. More effective steps are to be taken by the government for equipping the visually disabled with the needs of the time.

[74]This information is gathered from District Disabled and Senior Citizens Welfare Office based on the circular by name 'Arivina Sinchan' published by Karnataka State Government Disabled and Senior Citizens Department for facilities provided as an awareness programme.

gold, silver and bronze medals. The prize money ranges from Rs. 25 lakhs to Rs. 25,000 respectively. Presently the State Government encourages the visually impaired to be part of various games including cricket under BCCI which is a great achievement. As of now, all the schemes and programmes for sports are being implemented under the repealed PWD Act, 1995 which needs to be relooked at the earliest.

Finally, under section 80 of the RPWD Act of 2016, the State Commissioner was asked to recommend any suggestions or any provisions of any law or policy and programme and procedures which are inconsistent with this newly enacted RPWD Act of 2016. On behalf of the State Government the Commissioner was of the view that the State Government is expecting adequate funds, expertise training and technological devices from the Central Government. Holding the responsible position State Commissioner is expecting the State Universities and Law Universities in particular to contribute through their curricular studies, research, assignments and university level debates, conferences and seminars to spread general and legal awareness on the rights and duties of the disabled and the non-disables rights and duties towards the disables in the society. The fundamental education system therefore, should include the problems faced by the disabled in the society and the rights which they possess to lead a normal life with the other able people in the society. The support provided by the parents and guardians of the disabled children plays a imminent role in shaping the personality of their children. Support could be extended to them by providing training programmes for the parents of the disabled, the most resourceful persons, for the development of their disabled children which will help in creating legal awareness in their children and thereby, enabling them to recognize their rights in the society and to create a sense of belonging with their able bodied peer groups.

In the district level the Dharwad District Disabled and Senior Citizens Welfare Department is responsible for the administration of both persons with disabilities and the senior citizens.

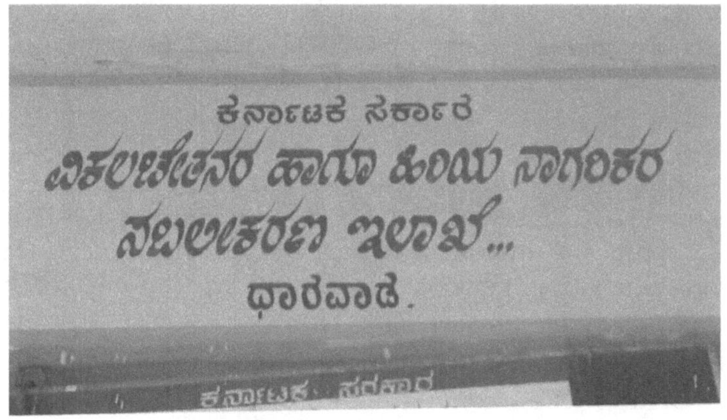

Fig. 2: Dharwad District Disabled and Senior Citizens Welfare Department

The disabled and senior citizens welfare officer shared his views regarding the implementation of the State government schemes in the district level as per the state governments notification and circulars. According to him, currently few schemes framed by the State government for the blind persons for the year 2017-18 includes providing of (i) identity card for 40 % visually impaired or above (ii) food and living allowance of Rs. 500 per month for 40 % category and 1200 per month for 75% and above (iii) scholarship for school and college students ranging from Rs. 1000/- to Rs 6000/-. (iv) Fee Reimbursement for students continuing their higher education after 10th Standard (v) competitive examination for appearing in IAS, KAS, FDC, SDC, Banking etc., (vi) Grants to NGOs running special schools for visually impaired (vii) Braille test books from 1st to 10th standard on concessional/ free rates (viii) talking laptop after 10th standard for their assistance in further studies (ix) free devises for visually impaired (x) interest free loans up to 20,000/- for their self employment (xi) special provision for visually impaired woman and students in matters of residential training and studies at concessional rates or at free of cost (xii) employment opportunities such as computer training, hardware training, data entry, DTP, DCAC courses for call centers and similar industrial jobs within the States(xiii) free bus and rail passes for 100% visually impaired persons and those having more than 40% and below 100% categories are provided at concessional rates (xiv) child allowance for 2years after delivery of 2 children an amount of Rs. 2000/- per month for the blind woman (xv) State level award programmes for persons or institutions serving for the disabled.

The implementation mechanisms under the Centre, State and District levels compel one to analyse the approach of the judiciary in recognizing the rights of the disabled in the society.

2.6 Judicial Approach in recognizing the rights of the disabled

Judiciary has always shown its concern towards creating awareness among the persons with disabilities and thereby, recognizing their rights in all spheres of life. The courts have interpreted the provisions of the legislations in most of the cases by upholding the sanctity of their humanitarian values towards recognizing the rights of persons with disabilities. Their concern is reflected in many of the decisions.

In the *Disabled Rights Group and Anr. v. Union of India and Others*[75] the Apex has given widest interpretation to

---

[75]Writ Petition (Civil) No. 997 of 2013, The three issues raised in the case are (i) non-implementation of 3% reservation of seats in educational institutions as provided in Sec. 39 of the PWD Act, 1995 and Sec. 32 of the RPWD, 2016. (ii) to provide proper access to orthopaedic disabled persons so that they are able to freely move in the educational institution and access the facilities (iii)Third issue pertains to pedagogy i.e. making adequate provisions and facilities of teaching for disabled persons, depending upon the nature of their disability, to enable them to undertake their studies effectively.

the provisions of the RPWD Act, 2016 by accepting the suggestions of the petitioner in the above case which is worthy to be highlighted in the light of inadequate infrastructure prevailing in most of the educational institutions for the disabled. The above case is elaborated as follows:

The petitioner brought to the notice of the court the guidelines framed by the University Grants Commission (UGC) for development grants to the colleges, wherein, the UGC has specifically made provisions concerning 'schemes for persons with disabilities'. There is a specific scheme with respect to Higher Education for Persons with Special Needs (HEPSN).

HEPSN scheme has three components, namely,

(i) Establishment of enabling units for differently-abled persons. The function of this unit as enumerated therein, includes creating awareness about the needs of differently-abled persons and other general issues concerning their learning. This special unit is to be guaranteed by a faculty member to be nominated by the Head of the Institution.

(ii) Component 2 of the scheme deals with providing access to differently-abled persons. For this purpose, UGC agreed to make a one-time grant of up to Rs.5 lakhs per college during the Plan period. To enable these institutions to make special arrangements in the environment for their mobility and independent functioning and to ensure that all existing structures as well as future construction projects in their campuses are made disabled friendly.

(iii) Third component deals with providing special equipment to augment educational services for differently-abled persons. It recognises that differently-abled persons require special aids and appliances for their daily functioning and that the higher educational institutes may need special learning and assessment devices in this behalf. In addition, visually challenged students need Readers. Thus, colleges are encouraged to procure such devices such as computers with screen reading software, low-vision aids, scanners, mobility devices etc.

Thus, the petitioner in the case had filed a compilation on February 22, 2016 containing suggestions, in the form of guidelines, insofar as making adequate infrastructure for providing proper access and also teaching facilities (Pedagogy) for differently-abled persons. They are as follows:

(I) INFRASTRUCTURE

(a) University/College Campus

Barrier-free campus environment according to the provisions of Sec. 45 and Sec. 46 of the Persons with Disability Act, 1995[76] and further according to 2001 guidelines issued by the Chief Commissioner for Persons with Disabilities entitled "Planning a Barrier Free Environment "[77]

(b) On Campus Accommodation

Regarding on campus accommodation (i) priority in the allotment of college hostel accommodation wherein, rooms should be preferably in the ground floor (ii) suitable room and bathroom modifications in hostel such as provision of ramps and special fittings/adjustable furniture to facilitate mobility and comfort (iii) availability of /helper / assistant, as required, to help the disabled student with mobility and

---

[76]The suggestions were made prior to the repeal of 1995 Act.

[77]Some specific examples are where a building is of more than 2 storeys, mandatory provision for lifts, straight and barrier-free paths, removal of obstacles such as plants, furniture or bicycles adjacent to doors, entrances, on the steps or in corridors. Unnecessary interior decoration of areas should be avoided where the same leads to impairment of the mobility of disabled persons.

orientation in hostel (iv) Special on-campus transportation on need basis. When on-campus accommodation is not provided (i) scheme for financial assistance to the disabled student for meeting expenses for off-campus accommodation and (ii) related requirements such as helper/attendant, transport to/from campus, etc.

(c) Classroom

For visually impaired – Braille symbols at appropriate places in classroom buildings to assist with orientation, auditory signals in elevators and lifts leading to classrooms to be installed. For students with low vision, adequate lighting in the classroom via natural light or adequate provision of bulbs, tube lights, etc has to be made. Making provision for recording of lectures, power plug points for visually impaired students to fit in their aids and appliances such as audio recorder, laptop, computer etc. is to be made. Classroom acoustics is to be designed in such a way that all audio communication is clearly audible.

(d) Science Laboratories

Need for structure and layout modifications of the laboratories for safety and comfort of the visually impaired and orthopaedic impaired/wheelchair users. There should be use of braille instruction sheets and tactile visual materials, availability of assistants for help with laboratory activities, particularly where some risk is involved, such as handling of chemicals, Sign language interpreters for hearing impaired.

(e) Libraries

For visually impaired students the libraries with well equipped braille section and fully accessible computer systems with scanning facilities, JAWS software and Braille embossers for printing. Again for low vision students there should be availability of large print books and computers equipped with text enlarging software, digital libraries and library cataloguing on computer with JAWS.

(f) Pedagogy

For visually impaired course material should be in accessible formats such as braille, audio books and also the electronic formats such as e-files in 'daisy' format. Easy availability of readers, note takers, scribes and suitable curriculum modification and assistance provided especially for scientific/ pictorial/graphical material and science laboratories, computers with screen reading software, accessible library and reference materials and availability of tape recorders/ digital voice recorders.

(g) Examination and Testing Modifications

These include the extension of time, use of reader/scribe, use of computer/laptop availability of question papers in accessible formats, including large print, braille, audio, daisy format, option of writing exams on computer with screen reading software, modification of pictorial and graphical material for visually impaired.

(h) University/College Administration

Facilitating for scribes, helpers and sign language interpreters for disabled students in interacting with university/ college administration, especially for the admission process, meetings with staff/ principal, on-campus company recruitment interviews and communication with college officials such as career counsellors, student counsellors, psychologists and any other person attached to the university/college who provides services of any type to the students. There is also need for special admissions window for disabled students and sensitivity training on disability to administrative and pedagogic staff.

(i) Sports, Culture, Recreation and Leisure Facilities

Universities/colleges need to ensure that cultural/ recreational programs take into account the needs of students with disabilities to provide for their full participation in such programs.[78] Special sporting events such as cricket to be conducted for visually impaired. International norms are to be modified to suit the needs of the disabled students and need to sensitize the trainers towards disability and inclusion and respective societies/associations to ensure that the information about events/contests reaches the disabled students. Similarly, adequate modifications are to be made available in cultural activities.[79]

Based on the aforesaid suggestions, the petitioner made written submissions on February 22, 2016, seeking following directions :[80]

(a) To ensure that 3% reservation for persons with disabilities in educational institutions are complied with including the backlog.

(b) To inspect all institutions of higher education to ensure that these institutions are made disable friendly

(c) To consider the "Guidelines for Accessibility for Students with Disabilities in Universities/Colleges" submitted by the petitioner pursuant to the order of this Court dated December 09, 2010."

After coming into force of the RPWD 2016, further directions are sought in tune with the provisions contained in the said Act by the court in this case in the following manner:

(d) To frame the rules for persons with disabilities[81] laying

---

[78]Some specific examples in sports: running courses/tracks to be straight where visually impaired and orthopaedic impaired students are participating.

[79]For example, disabled students are to be enabled to take part in theatre, literary, dance and music activities with the help of assistants.

[81]For an order directing the UGC for points a, b, and c and for an order directing the Central Government for points mentioned in d, e and f.

down the standards of accessibility for colleges, universities and other higher educational institutions, including pedagogical measures such as reasonable accommodation, modifications and aids and appliances for lectures, curricula, teaching materials, laboratories, libraries, examinations, classrooms and hostels etc. within six months from today; and for a direction to the appropriate governments to implement the said rules within two years from the notification of the said Rules in accordance with Sec. 46.

(e) To take into consideration the guidelines for accessibility for students with disabilities in Universities/Colleges, as submitted by the petitioner while framing the Rules under Section 40[82] of the Act

(f) To create an audit template in conformity with the Rules for accessibility in higher educational institutions.

(g) To invite applications from higher educational institutions for funding under the various schemes for accessibility and to release funds in accordance thereof to facilitate accessibility measures in the educational institutions.[83]

(h) To make their institutions accessible in accordance with the Act and the Rules within two years of the notification of the rules; and for mandatory formation in each institution of the Enabling Unit for disabled students as per UGC scheme 'HEPSN' to ensure monitoring and implementation of the standards and guidelines contained in the Rules.[84]

(i) To monitor the implementation of the Act and Rules and the orders of this Court to ensure compliance by

---

[82]Sec. 40 deals with accessibility for persons with disabilities

[83]This is for an order directing the UGC, the Central and the State Governments.

[84]This is for an order directing all higher educational institutions to comply with.

Central Government and State Advisory board.

The directions which are sought by the petitioners were in consonance with the provisions contained in the Disabilities Act, 2016. In these circumstances, the court disposed of this writ petition accepting the guidelines suggested by the petitioner along with its own other directions suitable as per the provisions of the Act of 2016.

Earlier in *Justice Sunanda Bhandare Foundation v. Union of India & Anr*[85] Supreme Court issued directions to the Central Government., State Governments and Union Territories to implement the provisions of the Persons with Disabilities (Equal Opportunities, Protection of Rights and Full Participation) Act, 1995 in the letter and spirit. On 19.7.2006, Supreme Court directed the Union and State Governments to file their responses in the form of affidavits within a period of four weeks wherein, some States filed their response and some have not.

In January 28, 2018 Supreme Court bench of justices Arun Mishra and S Abdul Nazeer again granted three months time to all States and Union territories to implement the RPWD Act 2016. The bench, which asked them to file the compliance report in three months, passed the order after Advocate Manali Singhal, representing the petitioner NGO-Sunanda Bhandare Foundation submitted that some States and UTs have filed affidavits saying that they have implemented 1995 Act but the Apex Court's verdict was for the amended Act. She cited that one third of the States in India including Karnataka failed to file affidavit wherein, court had asked all States to 'scrupulously' follow the 2016 law on the rights of

---

[85]Writ Petition (Civil) No. 116 of 1998,the writ petition was filed by justice Sunanda Bhandare Foundation, a charitable trust seeking (i) for implementation of the provisions of PWD Act, 1995 (ii) direction for reservation of 1% of the identified teaching posts in the faculties and college of various Universities under Art. 33 of PWD Act (iii) for declaration that denial of appointment to the visually disabled persons in the faculties and colleges of various Universities in the identified posts is violative of their fundamental right under Art. 14 and 15 read with Art. 41 of the Constitution.

persons with disabilities, saying it reflected "a sea change" in the perception of the Government on the critical issue. The court said the States and the union territories must realize that under the new Act their responsibilities have increased and the executing authorities must give effect to it with "quite promptitude".[86]

Summing Up

The implementation of 2016 Act is not easy unless the government frames rules for all the implementing provisions. The government has given an assurance on equality, non-discrimination on the ground of disability unless it is shown that the impugned act or omission is a proportionate means of achieving a legitimate aim. However, there is no clarity as to the implementation of education, social security, free health care etc., Above all, it is disheartening to know that there is lack of exact statistics for persons with disabilities. Presently, government has announced a survey covering persons with 21 disabilities and has also earmarked 5 Crore for it which is indeed a welcome note. But what is required is that the survey should be a proper socio-economic one to be done scientifically.[87] Again, for disability certificates, the certifying authority under the Act is to give disability certificates[88] and accordingly every district government

[86]Prabhati Nayak Mishra, "Proper Implementation of Rights of Persons with Disabilities Act, 2016: SC grants three months' time for States and UTs", www.livelaw.in ,January 28, 2018 7:34 PM

[87]K.C. Deepika, Karnataka Budget: Survey of Persons with Disabilities announced, *The Hindu*, 6th July, 2018.

[88]According to Dr. Sunil Gokhale, Lecturer in community Medicine, KIMS, the disability certificate is issued to persons with disabilities mentioned in the PWD Act, 1995. In order to get a disability certificate a person requires a birth certificate and a proof of residence. However, Medical Boards in many hospitals set up for this purpose are not working. These certificates are issued as per the temporary (reversible) impairedness and permanent (non-reversible) impairedness. In temporary impairedness the certificates are issued according to the span of time the relative illness is cured such as on completion of successful surgery in the head or brain affected area within 1 or less than 10 years by which there are chances of recovery of impairedness of the eyes. If the certificates are not mentioned with specific year(s)/ span of time, then it will be assumed that the certificates are valid for 10 years and needs to be renewed before or on the time of its expiry.

hospital and medical colleges if any, are designated to be the certifying authorities in respective States. Presently under the Karnataka Government, Karnataka Medical College (KMC) and the Dharwad District hospital has been designated as the certifying authorities for the visually disabled in the Hubballi-Dharwad area. However, the disability certificate issued by the authorities will be valid only in the respective States and the requirement as of now is the universal validity for disability certificates. The percentage of financial allocation is also still doubtful. Although the government has passed the law unless there is support for budgetary allocation, it cannot be implemented.[89] The 2016 Act has various provisions which require huge allocation of money. In the Union budget 2018 statement and speech, there is no mention for budgetary allocation for implementation of Three Year Action plan for the disabled people.[90] Many more issues are still to be resolved in the implementation of the Act which casts an onerous duty on respective State governments.

[89]The budget in its "miserly outlay" allocated Rs 300 crore towards the Schemes for the Implementation of the Persons with Disabilities Act (SIPDA) which provides financial assistance for implementation.

[90]Disability Rights Activists say Jaitley's budget a 'big disappointment', *Indian Express*, New Delhi, September 28, 2018.

CHAPTER 3

EMPIRICAL STUDY ON VISUALLY DISABLED IN HUBBALLI-DHARWAD AREA

Karnataka State lying in the southern part of India has an enthralling history of its own. The State enriched with the distinctive culture and values has been under the rule of several dynasties that have shaped its history. For a long time the State was under the British rule before it gained independence. The period 1905 to 1920 is described as the period of unification of Karnataka wherein, on one hand, when there was struggle to release India from the clutches of British rule, on the other hand, the freedom fighters dreamt of building a united Karnataka State.[91] However, the State of Karnataka was formed only on November 1, 1956 under the State Reorganisation Act, 1956 and later with the relentless work of great men of the time the State, originally known as State of Mysore, was renamed as Karnataka on November 1, 1973. Located in the western part of the Indian peninsula the State lies between 11.5° and 19° north latitudes and 74° and 78° east latitudes. The Hubballi-Dharwad is the second largest city in the State of Karnataka and is separated by a distance of 20 kms. The population of Hubballi was very low before independence. However, there was a steady rise in the population from 1961 to 1981which started declining from 1981. In 1991the growth rate was 28.42% and thereafter, declined to 18.65% during 2001. Lack of development in trade and commerce and other related economic activities was

---

[91]Karnataka has been a land of freedom fighters from earlier times and have seen and witnessed decisive battles fought by brave men of the State like Hyder Ali, Tippu Sultan of Mysore, Rani Channamma of Kittur, Sangolli Rayanna of Bailhongal,Bheema Rao of Mundaragi and many more....

the main cause of such decline. On the contrary, Dharwad witnessed an improved growth rate during 1961 to1981, but again during 1991-2001, the growth rate was only 26.33%. As per the city development plan the population of the city is expected to grow up to 12 lakh in 2021 and 15 lakh in 2031, with expected growth rate of 47 to 62 % in 2021 and 62 to 76% in 2031.[92] As per 2011 Census, Hubballi- Dharwad has a total population of 943788 (Nine Lakhs Forty Three Thousand Seven Hundred and Eighty Eight) of which male and female are 474,518 and 469,270 respectively.[93]

India has identified the major causes of blindness as cataract, trachoma, malnutrition, infections, glaucoma etc., and has also realized that these causes are largely preventable or curable with currently available knowledge and skills. However, there is gross inadequacy of qualified ophthalmologists and availability of services in the rural area. Another contributory cause of incidence of preventable blindness is the lack of knowledge and concern on the part of large segments of the population about the nature and causes of blindness and possible and available preventive measures and services.[94] The disability certificate, the basic document that a person with any disability of more than 40% requires in order to avail any facilities, benefits or concessions under the available schemes, however, this is not a requirement for getting admission in a school for formal education. Presently, under the Karnataka Government, Karnataka Medical College (KMC) and the Dharwad District hospital has been designated as the certifying authorities for the visually disabled in the Hubballi-Dharwad area. The criteria for the issue of disability certificate based on the categories of visual

[92]Government of India, Ministry of Urban Development, Service Level Benchmark, Urban Transport, http://www.utbenchmark.in (last updated Dec.7, 2018)

[93]Hubballi and Dharwad City Census 2011 data see http://www.census2011.co.in

[94]Dr. B.V. Subrahmanyam's, *Law and Practice of Disability Consequent to Medical Negligence including Human Disability Evaluation of Personal Injuries, Principles, Practice and Law,* (Allahabad: Practice and Law, Law Publishers (India) Ltd, 2008).

disability by KMC is provided in Table: 3

Table 3 : Categories of visual disability as updated by KIMS

Category	Better Eye	Worse Eye	% Impairment
0	6/9 – 6/18	6/24 – 6/36	20%
I	6/18 – 6/36	6/60 – Nil	40%
II	6/40 – 4/60 Or Field of Vision 10^0– 20^0	3/60 – Nil	75%
III	3/60 – 1/60 Or Field of Vision 10^0	F.C. at 1 Ft. to Nil	100%
IV	F.C. at 1 Ft. to Nil Or Field of Vision 10^0	F.C. at 1 Ft. to Nil	100%
V	One eyed Person	F.C. at 1 Ft. to Nil of Vision 10^0	30%

Source : Primary data

3.1 Institutions for visually impaired in Hubballi-Dharwad Area

The blind schools, other institutions and NGOs working for the blind are scattered in Hubballi- Dharwad is listed in Table 4: and the study on the following Governmental and Non-Governmental institutions reveals their extent of legal awareness of the new legislation i.e. the Act of 2016 which are listed as follows:

Government Residential Educational Institutions			Non-Governmental Organisations		
Sl No.	Name	Area of Functioning	Sl No.	Name	Area of Functioning
1	Blind boys Govt. residential school, Siddharoodmath, Hubballi	Residential School	1	Chikenkoppad Shree Chennaveer Sharanara's Welfare Ashram for Blind, Hubballi	provides residence to visually disabled and non-disabled male children from poor and backward community
2	Shri Aarooda Education Society's For Blind Residential School, Hubballi	Residential School	2	Samarthanam Trust For The Disabled, Dharwad	Providing quality education, accommodation, nutritious food, vocational training, sports and placement based rehabilitation
			3	Sahana Charitable Trust For The Disabled, Dharwad	Braille books transcription Centre

Source : Primary data

3.1.1 Government Residential Educational Institutions

- Government Residential School for Blind Boys, Siddharoodmath, Hubballi:

Established in the year 1955 as a residential school for blind boys from 1st standard to 7th standard, the school is situated in Hubballi near the historical and holy place of Siddharoodmath[95] and has a peaceful atmosphere suitable for visually disabled children.

Fig. 3: Blind Boys Government Residential School, Hubballi

<u>Staff:</u>

The sanctioned staff members for the school is 17 and currently 7 are employed and rest of the 10 posts are still vacant. As of now there are four teaching staff who are handling music courses and normal curriculum. The following table 5 explains the working and vacant positions.

---

[95]The school is known in the name of the great saint Shri Siddharudha Swamy who was an advaita yogi and believed all people equal disregarding the caste system.

Table 5: Staffs in Blind Boys Government Residential School, Hubballi

Sr. No.	Posts	Sanctioned	Filled up	Vacant (Since)
1	Superintended (Gazetted Group B, Class II Officer	1	-	1(2013)
2	Undergraduate Teacher (Special D.Ed) (Group C)	3	2	1 (2005)
3	Braille teacher (Special D.Ed) (Group C)	1	-	1 (2017)
4	Music Teacher Grade II (Group C)	2	2	-
5	Orientation and Mobility Teacher (Group C)	1	-	1 (1955)
6	Warden (S.S.L.C.) and special training (Group C)	1	1	-
7	Second Division Clerk (Group C)	1	1	-
8	Cook (Group D)	1	-	1 (2014)
9	Peons (Group D)	3	-	3 (2011, 2015, 2016)
10	Hostel Servant (Group D)	1	-	1 (1988)
11	Night Watchman (Group D)	1	1	-
12	Sweeper (Group D)	1	-	1 (2017)
	Total	17	7	10

Source : Primary data

The most important and required post of Orientation and Mobility trainer who trains to develop the other senses of the blind student remains vacant since 1955. The post of the Warden has been filled not in accordance with the norms and eligibility of the post. Braille teachers important for educational development are also vacant since 2017. Apart from this, hostel servant and sweeper post also remains vacant which are posing threats on hygiene, maintenance of the institutional premises and educational development arenas.[96] Additional required posts to be sanctioned as per the requirement of the school are as follows:

1. Office Superintendent one Post;

2. First Division Clerk;

3. Head Master;

4. Warden specially for House-keeping; and

5. Laundry

Every month the report of vacancy of staff along with other requirements are submitted but prompt action is yet to be taken regarding filling up of the vacancies. Senior teacher and acting Head Master of the school[97] was only aware of the repealed PWD Act, 1995 but not on the new legislation of 2016. He is aware of basic rights under the Indian Constitution and Human Rights, discrimination on the grounds of disability, rights of disabled persons and more in particular about blind persons. He also expressed his willingness to know more on the rights and laws for disabled persons. He shared his experience on the pros and

---

[96]The post of cook has not been filled but has been outsourced since 2014 on temporary basis. Vacancy of three posts of Peons is pending since 2011, 2015 and 2016 (after the death of two peons and one peon being retired).

[97]Mr. Annappa Koli is the senior most teacher who is also the acting head master of the school having around 31 years of professional experience. He is also a mentor for Balaparadhi Unit (Juvenile justice home) in Bellary from 1987 till 2008 and from 2008 till present. Since last 10 years he is working as a senior teacher in the present boys blind school. He has pursued his M.A. in Mathematics and M.Ed. in special education from IGNOU.

cons of the residential blind school education and its actual implementation in Karnataka.

Education:

The visually blind children are studying the same syllabus as that of the non disabled peers and the study materials are available for them in Braille. In case of any changes or corrections to be made in the study material of the blind children the teaching staff gets it rectified through the government run publishing press which is located only at Mysore.

The result of the school for the year 2017 -2018 is 91.66 % which was lagging behind only because of non appearance of students in the exams after taking their admissions. The strength of students have varied every year due to parents/ guardians and/or their children's wish and they are continuing their education only with the frequent counseling of the institution head.

This casts an obligation on the part of the government and duty of educational institutions as per section 16 (vii) of the RPWD Act of 2016 in matters concerning monitoring of the students participation.[98]

Environmental Barriers and accessibility:

The institution lacks barrier free environment with respect to accessibility and mobility of the blind children. However, Rs.3 Crore has been sanctioned by State Government and deposited for new and modern building which is under construction since 2010.

Rehabilitation, health and recreation:

---

[98]As per Sec 16(viii) of the RPWD Act, 2016, The appropriate Government and the local authorities shall endeavor that all educational institutions funded or recognised by them provide inclusive education to the children with disabilities and towards that end shall monitor participation, progress in terms of attainment levels and completion of education in respect of every student with disability.

School gets donations from the public in the form of teaching materials, bed, clothes etc., Devotees are also allowed to donate cooked food and to feed the children with their own hands which is considered as part of social service.

Health and other facilities of all blind children in the school are taken care by government hospitals located in old Hubballi. In the month of June these children are provided with free check up.

The school has purchased and is also donated with musical instruments such as harmonium and tabla for their students along with their normal curriculam. The school utilizes them also in the social and religious ceremonies and functions in their spare time.

- Shri Aarooda Education Society's Residential School for Blind, Hubballi:

Established in the year 2000 Shri Aarooda Education Society's School for Blind is again a residential school for blind girls from 1st standard to 10th standard and for blind boys from 8th standard to 10th standard.[99] The school is also located at the holy place of Siddharoodmath, Hubballi within a distance of one kilometer from Blind Boys Residential School, Siddharoodmath, Hubballi.

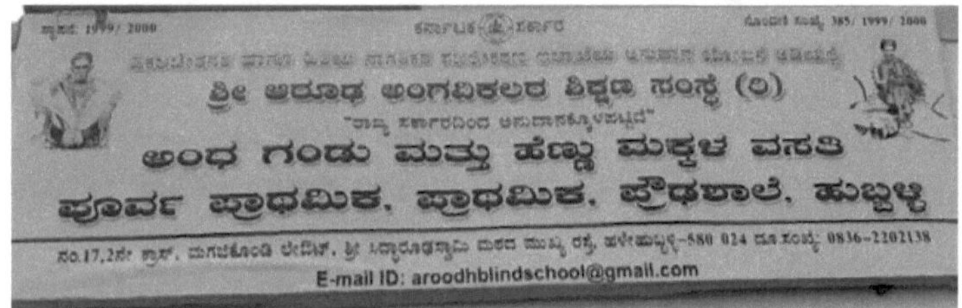

**Fig. 4: Shri Aaroodha Disabled's (Blind Residential School
for Boys and Girls)**

---

[99]They provide co-education with blind girls.

<u>Staff:</u>

All the posts of staff members including teaching and non-teaching members are filled every year as per the requirement. Currently 17 teaching and 13 non-teaching staffs are working for the welfare of the blind students.

<u>Environmental Barriers and accessibility:</u>

Head Mistress of the school shared her experience in the interview with her on the attitude of parents and guardians as against the benefits and opportunities provided by the State government. The need to create legal awareness on the parents and the blind students was emphasized by the School authorities since inception. However, the authorities themselves revealed the lack of legal awareness and interest of parents and guardians in providing education for their visually disabled children and also expressed their desire to get better opportunities in their struggle for recognition of their rights. According to her, because of the two conflicting views as to educate their children and the lack of awareness to procure the same in a barrier free and healthy environment, parents themselves feel more secure[100] in the existing situation to have their visually impaired children with them in their own home rather than getting educated in a residential school reasonably far or near from their place of residence. The insecurity expressed by the parents of female child becomes more relevant in the light of the increasing sexual offences against children in the society.

<u>Health:</u>

Free health care is provided by the Government hospital located at old Hubballi. Eye checkups are also regularly conducted by govt. doctors every year in the month of June. With the assistance of Rotary club and inner wheel club,

---

[100] The parents expressed their genuine anxiety as to the security of their visually disabled children (both boy and girl) in the residential schools itself.

private institutions, are also organising dental check up camps, and other health related check-ups for the children.

<u>Recreation:</u>

Apart from studies music, quiz on general knowledge is arranged for the children for their holistic development. For national festivals the students are allowed to celebrate the occasion in their residence with their family members if declared to be a national holiday by the State govt. Apart from national holidays on all national celebrations such as Republic day, Independence day flag hosting is performed along with other events arranged for the occasion. Recently Gandhi Jayanthi was celebrated in the school on October 2nd wherein, all the students enthusiastically participated. Other cultural activities such as gathering, get together, saraswathi pooja and other religious celebrations are arranged by the schools with the active participation of the children. Trips are organized for the students annually free of cost. [101]The school has earlier organized trips outside the State like Kolapur, Pune, Shiradi etc.,

<u>Rehabilitation:</u>

The Society receives old news papers from the people who are aware of its use in such blind schools. Though limited in number these old news papers are used for braille learning of the blind children[102] in their regular class room learning. The office receives correspondence on disability matters from the department of Empowerment of Disabled and Senior

---

[101]Recently in this year the school had a trip to Kolluru Mukambike, Udupi and surrounding places.

[102]There were many earlier and vivid forms of embossed writing for the blind. It was only the beginning of the 20th Century that general acceptance was given to the superiority of Braille's system by reason of its simplicity and the speed and ease with which it can be written. The development of Braille from simple notion used by a few blind students in one institution into a universal system of reading and writing is the result of international cooperation and very soon it penetrated every linguistic area due to combined efforts of the educators who were establishing blind schools throughout the world and the missionaries who wanted to make the scriptures available to the blind.

Citizens, Dharwad. District Disabled's Welfare Officer, is in charge of any enquiry, inspection or investigation of the school in general for its proper functioning and management.[103] Any proposal of school will be sent to him for his approval. District Children's Protection Committee visits for inspection once annually or twice on any other occasion as per the orders from the higher authorities.

3.1.2 Non-Governmental Residential Institutions

- Chikenkoppad Shree Chennaveer Sharanara's Welfare Ashram for Blind, Hubballi:

Established in the year 2000, Chikenkoppad Shree Chennaveer Sharanara's Welfare Ashram is a private trust run by Shree Shivashanth Virasharanaru[104] who is also the honorable President for the trust. The trust consists of nine members as trustees along with the President. The Ashram is a non-governmental aided institution and is also run on donations from devotees.[105] It provides residence to visually disabled and non-disabled male children from poor and backward community.

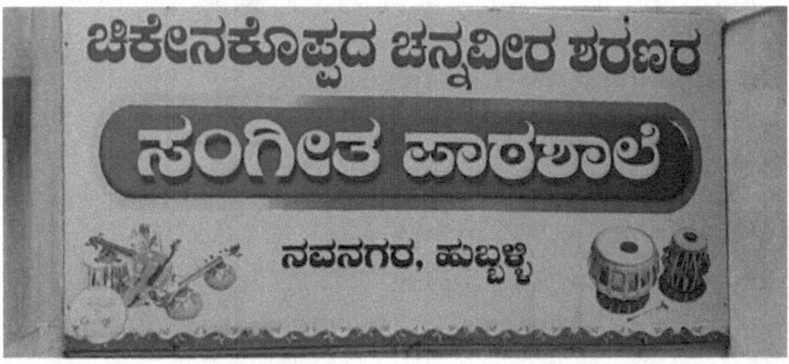

Fig. 5: Chikenkoppad Shree Chennaveer Sharanara's Music School, Hubballi

[103]Mr. Amarnath K.M., District Disable's Welfare Officer

[104]Shree Shivashanth Virasharanaru is a spiritual divotee indulging himself for the social cause of the society.

[105]The Trust is managed by Mr. Shankarayya V. Hiremath.

<u>Staff</u>

The manager of the trust, who being a teacher himself along with other teachers constitutes the staff of the Ashram. Therefore, as of now there are only two teachers and two cooks. Currently there are 26 visually disabled and 16 non-disabled students residing in the Ashram.

<u>Health, recreation and rehabilitation:</u>

Since 2000 fifty beneficiaries of the Ashram are placed in government departments and the trust is even supporting financially their beneficiaries for preparation in competitive examinations including UPSC exams. It is also financially assisting their beneficiaries in their Pre-primary education till their Post graduation and further studies free of cost by way of payment of fees through their trust.

Ashram provides food in the form of prasadam and other basic needs of life to the visually disabled and non-disabled male children from poor and backward community. It also provides medical facilities free of cost.

The Trust also imparts musical education, education on astrology and performance of other religious rituals like Homa, Havana, Rudrakshamantra chanting, Namakarana poojas and thus helps in the holistic development of the inmates along with their skill development and spirituality in terms of preserving the tradition of Hindu rituals through these beneficiaries. This involvement will in turn help them in future with their way of livelihood.

• Samarthanam Trust for the Disabled, Dharwad:

A national award winning NGO established in the year 1997, Samarthanam Trust For The Disabled was founded by Mahantesh G. Kivadasannavar and Nagesh S.P. Samarthanam who themselves being blind and thereby, decided to lead the blind through this NGO. Samarthanam serves the blind disabled people free of cost as well as abled people with a minimal fee for the services availed by them in the form of providing quality education, accommodation, nutritious food, vocational training, sports and placement based rehabilitation.[106]

Fig. 6: Samarthanam Trust , Dharwad Office

Staff:

The Samarthanam Trust Dharwad office has 25 staff members which include: one male non-disabled B.P.O. trainer, one female non-disabled English and communication trainer and one female visually disabled computer skill trainer[107] and the rest on skill development and operations as supporting staffs. Apart from this, the Regional Manager manages to get volunteers from various educational institutions who voluntarily serve the motive of the trust on occasional events whole heartedly.

Education:

Dharwad branch is currently imparting the Information Technology and Business Process Outsourcing Training for disabled and has future plans of imparting Banking and Insurance training which is already initiated in Bangalore

[106]Revansiddayya G. S. is in charge of the Trust's management as Regional Manager for Dharwad Division and as North Karnataka Head in terms of co-ordination for any events in these region.

[107]The female staff has completed her special teacher's training from Mysore which is the only training centre for computer teacher's training programme in Karnataka

branch. Specifically for visually disabled beneficiaries the trust has facilitated various instruments, applications and means to impart education in academics, music and other skill developments.

The educational syllabus is converted from visual literature to MP3 audio for better and convenient understanding. Such converted audio is compiled in gadgets like I-pod and are provided free of cost to the visually impaired students. The computer training is imparted through the help of Job Access with Speech (JAWS technology).

Recreation:

Musical instruments are also provided free of cost. To recreate the positive atmosphere, the trust organizes talent shows on every Friday for disabled to showcase their talents. All the beneficiaries are allowed to bring their friends, families to share joy, have fun, and be part of its noble cause.

Rehabilitation:

In addition, Samarthanam provides hostel, food and medical facilities free of cost for both genders. The visually impaired students are assisted to get Scholarship programmes wherein, the amount accrued will be credited directly in their account. They also facilitate volunteers to be scribers for the needy disabled in their examinations.

J.S.S. Vidyagiri, Dharwad, K.C.D. Mahanth College and other few educational institutes have been tied up with the trust in order to get the disabled students continue their further studies after their matriculation. Good number of management students as volunteers from B.V.B. Campus, Hubballi frequently support in fund raising and event management services. These institutions have shown their full support in the Trust's struggle for further educating the disabled students who have completed their matriculation and are searching the options for their livelihood.

Usually the disabled after their matriculation are open to continue their further studies along with the non-disabled peers all over the globe. Here the Trust plays the role of motivator in exploring the zeal of these disabled children to choose the options of further studies or skill development in order to make their way of life and livelihood with confidence to match with the other able bodied peers.

3.1.3 Non-Governmental Braille Books Transcription Centre

• Sahana Charitable Trust for the Disabled, Dharwad:

Established in 2000, Sahana charitable trust is a Braille book transcription Centre that provides free Braille books for all blind students covering maximum regions of North Karnataka. Its main Office is located in Bangalore and branches are located in Mysore and Dharwad. The Dharwad branch was established in the year 2009.[108] The trust is serving the blind students in providing their academic literature through braille since 18 years. The Trust runs without any Government grants but only on the public donations. Apart from educational books it has its own braille library at its centre. The Dharwad centre has five employees including three visually blind.

Fig. 7: Sahana Charitable Trust and Braille Book Transcription Centre for the disabled, Dharwad

---

[108]The Co-ordinator is Mr. Ramachander Dhongade is in charge of the North Karnataka's first Braille library and citizen's reading room.

The Co-ordinator of the trust shared his efforts taken for the betterment of blind after their schooling and in their way for earning a livelihood. He revealed that the visually disabled are facilitated with education, educational materials and residence with other basic requirements of life under the established institutions of the Government. But after their schooling there are no arrangements made for the blind to procure braille literature for their further studies or skill development programmes from the government. To enhance the life of visually impaired apart from their usual educational literature, the trust has decided to publish and distribute a bi-monthly magazine named "Belaku" (Light) in Kannada braille language on subjects covering culture, legal, health, story, poems, sports, current affairs and matters relating to general knowledge for the visually impaired. The trust has decided to distribute this magazine to the 50 blind schools in the state free of cost. The Coordinator in his words expressed his anxiety by reflecting the non-cooperative attitude of the different departments of the State which is emphasized below.

(i)   In spite of Sahana's communication to 40 universities in the State regarding the collection of exact figures of the visually disabled in the State, Universities have not responded and supported to disclose their study material requirements nor the syllabus.

(ii) the trust has also offered the Universities to provide the required study materials free of cost for which most of the Universities has not responded

(iii) Although the trust expressed their willingness to the government officials and ministers in providing braille books free of cost for the college level and professional level students many a times, there is no communication from the governmental departments in this regard.

(iv) The library being North Karnataka's first Braille library and citizen's reading room having diverse reading materials on all fields of life for both blind and abled citizens it is rarely used and utilized for enhancing the knowledge.

For all these reasons, the trust has failed to collect the exact figures of visually disabled in the State. The lack of exact figures of visually impaired in the State has been brought to the notice of medical and primary education minister of Karnataka.

3.2 Other Institutions for the Visually Impaired in Hubballi-Dharwad

3.2.1 Non Governmental Organisations:

Civil society has always played an inevitable role in the protection and promotion of the rights of persons with disabilities. Their areas of action can be analysed under different heads namely (i) imparting education (ii) creating awareness and advocacy (iii) making aware of schemes and benefits of the schemes of the government (iv) securing social justice (v) establishing infrastructure (vi) community based rehabilitation (viii) livelihood programmes etc., In addition to the role played by NGOs the contribution of other institutions is also analysed in this section. Some NGOs in Hubballi-Dharwad and their contribution is listed below:

- Samadrishti Kshamata Vikas Evam Anusandhan Mandal (SAKSHAM):

Fig. 8: Samadrishti, Kshamata vikas evam Anusandhan Mandal (SAKSHAM)

SAKSHAM is a charitable national organization established with an aim to bring the persons with various disabilities in the main stream of the society. Though presently dedicated to the service of visually impaired, SAKSHAM has its commitment towards all the persons with disabilities and also on matters relating to environment, health and other social activities to strengthen the society. As of now, it does not have its registered office in Hubballi-Dharwad area but operates through its volunteers spread across the district and beyond. Presently, SAKSHAM is running various projects for integrated development of the disabled. Some of which are specified below:

Eye Bank and assistive devices for visually impaired

SAKSHAM propagates the importance and divinity of eye donation through its Madhav Eye Bank and manages the donation of corneas through eye banking and grafting to give sight for therapeutic purposes. It has successfully invented a device named AUDIO BOOK READER AND RECORDER which is first of its kind developed in our country and is presently being successfully used by more than 100 blind students personally and has been installed as Group Hearing Library Setup in some educational institutions including some colleges.

Cornea Andhatv Mukta Bharat Abhiyan(CAMBA)

CAMBA, an initiative of SAKSHAM aims to ascertain the actual number of persons affected by Corneal opacity and requiring restoration of sight from eye donation, diagnose the enlisted people for corneal opacity to analyze the possibility of relief through eye donation. The task is accomplished with the networking by Sight Keepers (Netra Rakshak) at grass root level. They even coordinate with the existing network of Eye Banks to start Eye Collection Centers. They propagate the need of Eye Donation through intense awareness amongst public thereby, taking efforts for improvement in the infrastructure for Eye donation in the country.

- National Association for the Blind (NAB)

NAB, an Indian origin NGO has its head office in Mumbai, Maharashtra. It has its branch in almost every State.[109] They conduct programs for the visually impaired by providing computer based training courses, development of communication skills, Training the trainers under the Program Train the Trainers, operating of digital library, providing employability oriented courses such as skill development and self-employment for visually impaired in Karnataka State.

The Mumbai head office has not imposed any restrictions on its State branches for any of its managing or operating decisions in the welfare of the blind in their own States. The organization runs on funds partially funded by the State and Central Governments, but the greater portion of funds is through the donations from members of public and private sectors. One of its training centres is run through the State Government aid wherein, the trainers are paid directly by the State Government. Fig. 8 depicts NAB, Bengaluru.

Fig. 9: NAB Karnataka branch

[109]M. Srinivas is the Chief Executive Officer of NAB Karnataka branch

NAB under its Train the trainers Program has plan to train 16 new instructors and establish new taluk level locations each year, but is lagging with financial support from public. NAB has approached many multi-national and national companies in Bangalore for donations and support and has been provided with assistance through their corporate social responsibility.

NAB has no centres in Dharwad district due to non-sponsorship and donations from neither the public nor from corporate sectors located there. It has plans to establish its operations in Dharwad and Belgaum with financial assistance and support from the public residing in those areas. NAB had worked in collaboration with Lions Club and Rotary Club in Hubballi for creating awareness on skills and training for blind and in turn Lions Club and Rotary Club have sponsored some visually impaired students from Dharwad District for training in NAB, Bangalore Centre.

Other services rendered by the organization are counseling visually impaired to face a period of intense training and about managing life and work as an independent individual, training on hygiene and personal and home management, mobility training covering the rules of walking in public using a cane, moving about in a room, negotiating steps and escalators, commuting in a bus and learning techniques to map and memorize routes and layouts, placement and post placement counseling.

On education, as NAB is mainly concerned with imparting technical skills and carrier development courses and not in primary, secondary and higher education they still have strong views on inclusive education which will be dealt in the next chapter.

NAB has won three national and one state award for its placement for visually impaired and making way for their life and living. Expecting more support in future from the Government and the public from every district including

Dharwad district NAB is looking forward to serve and establish their centers in every district of Karnataka to fulfill their mission of making the visually challenged equal members of society.

- National Federation of Blind (NFB)

NFB is a self help organization for the blind founded in 1970 with the philosophy "let the Blind lead the Blind". It is an Indian based NGO having its national and central office located at New Delhi.

Fig. 10: National Federation of the Blind, Karnataka Branch

NFB (Karnataka) was established on 10th July 2004 and has its principle office and Blind Braille cum talking library and assistive devices of aids and appliances supply service in Karnataka at Bangalore and regional units in Mysore and Hubballi.[110] As the issues are resolved online and communication is reached digitally, Hubballi unit has no formal physical office but as per the officials their members are active through mails and other modes of communication with the visually impaired in the city in resolving their concerned problems.

---

[110]NFB (Karnataka) has celebrated its 13th anniversary on 4th January 2018.

Fig. 11: NFB Residential and office Building

The governing Council of NFB is elected for five years and for the year 2016 to 2021 there are 15 members including the President, Vice President, General Secretary, Secretary, Treasurer and Co-ordinator. Except the treasurer all the members are visually impaired.

NFB is engaged in resolving all socio-economic problems of visually challenged persons such as basic needs, pension, social-security, medical certificates and all other Government provided facilities with the view to ensure them decent living with dignity and also to enable them to strive for enforcement, protection and promotion of all basic human rights of visually challenged population of the State. NFB has plans to reopen its unit physically in Hubballi and Belgaum to reach out the visually impaired population in the northern part of the State.[111]

Information and Counselling service:

Under this service federation manages to collect and disseminate accurate and updated information to the visually challenged individuals, their parents and institutions on various opportunities, facilities and benefits available to them in different fields of life from the public and private sector at International, National and State level.

[111]Information gathered through interview with the Manager of NFB

NFB makes available the copies of various notifications, circulars and judgments issued by the State governments, Central Government and judiciary for all type of benefits to persons with visual disability. It also offers counseling to the visually impaired persons regarding their carrier selection, workplace solution, legal consultation and social support.[112] Under this project the Federation publishes a fortnightly e-bulletin "Voice of the Blind" containing all latest news, announcements, job opportunities and related information for the visually impaired persons. At present the news paper is being circulated among 1000 individuals and institutions all over the country through email. Any interested person may subscribe this bulletin by providing just his/her mail ID.

NFB is also running an SMS service known as "NFB Job Alert" under which the availability of job openings anywhere in State or Central Government for persons with visual disability are disseminated through SMS. At present the SMS of job alert are circulated among 1000 subscribers in Karnataka and more than 500 in rest of India.

Any person who is willing to avail the benefits of this service may make a request to the General Secretary of the Federation to subscribe the service.

As a new initiative NFB has also started the publication of audio version of leading monthly Kannada Magazine "Spardhaspoorthi" which is very useful for preparation of competitive exams.

Each monthly issue of the magazine is made available to its subscribers on MP3CD at their door step just on a nominal subscription of Rs.100/- per annum. The magazine has also been uploaded on Sugamya Pustakalaya[113] for free download by the users.[114]

---

[112]For information see www.nfbkarnataka.org/services

[113]The NFB library is also member of Sugamya Pustakalaya, which is an on-line library and members of this library may have access to Sugamya Pustakalaya through this library.

[114]*National Federation of Blind Souvenir,*(Karnataka: NFB, 2018)

State level braille cum talking library:

The library has around 1,200 collections of books in three languages i.e. English, Hindi and Kannada. The subject of general interest which the library covers are history, health, geography, law, literature, disability study, general knowledge, women literature, child literature, competitive exams and other reference books. It also includes book from 12th standard and State level degree language text books.

NFB is providing Braille converted language text books to maximum Universities in the State except Bangalore at nominal rates. Bangalore University provides its own Braille Books to its visually impaired students. Every blind person across the State is entitled to take the membership of library just by making a payment of Rs.100 towards a life membership.

Aids and appliances services:

NFB Karnataka operates a store of wide range of assistive devices which are used by the blind persons in their day to day life. The store procures all such devices from reputed manufacturers and dealers across the country and abroad and makes them available to the visually challenged individuals and their institutions in the State at its actual cost. The assistive devices available at the store include braille learning and writing devices, mobility aids, educational aids, indoor and outdoor games, puzzles and personal devices.

Advocacy and Awarness:

The NFB Karnataka has devised a well focused programme of advocacy with the support of its national leaders and undertakes the initiative of both legal and civil advocacy in order to influence the government for improvement and modernization of public policies and practices governing the rehabilitation, education, employment, social security and other concerns of persons with disability in general and blind in particular.

It is also actively engaged in delivery of benefits of various welfare schemes of Central and State government to maximum number of people with visual disability in order to promote equality of this marginalized group, to reduce their exclusion, to help them in participating in all developmental measures, make them heard and assert their rights.

The Federation also initiates prompt action in discriminatory practices against the visually impaired persons which are brought to their notice either by an individual or an organization. On the initiative of the federation, various courts of law have given land mark decisions in order to recognize, protect and promote entitlements of the persons with disabilities.

The federation also persuades the State government for effective implementation of Persons with Disabilities Act 1995, (and now the Act of 2016) UN convention of the Rights of Persons with Disability and directions of the judiciary regarding socio-economic empowerment of persons with disability.

Further, the federation also undertakes regular awareness campaigns for publicizing the capabilities of visually impaired persons and is working in close cooperation with National Institute for Empowerment of Persons with Visual Disability and other national organizations for capacity building of Visually Impaired.

3.2.2 Financial Institutions:

- Nationalised public sector and private sector banks

Fig. 12: State Bank of India, Administrative Office, Hubballi

Visually impaired are allowed to open savings account in nationalized public and private sector banks along with co-applicants who may be family members or friends. Matters pertaining to sole account holding and current account opening, mortgage loan account, debit/credit card transactions are considered by the banks as per their lawyer's empanelment suggestions.

Sole account holders of savings account are however, not provided with the cheque book facility, but are given the option to visit the base branch along with the one who owes a debt from the visually impaired account holder. In such a situation, the visually impaired through a withdrawal slip filled by the banker authenticates the payer's legal capacity and intention to pay the debt amount.

In debit/credit card processing the maximum of ATM machines are installed with the braille system or are facilitated with identifiable indications for visually impaired account holders.

The bankers are guided as per the RBI Guidelines in all matters relating to an account holder who is visually impaired which may extent to making of alterations, modifications, refusals in terms of granting of loans, opening of accounts, issuance of debit and credit cards and other related legal matters where surety is involved.

The obligation of the bank to maintain confidentiality of its visually impaired account holders will be at par with their non disabled counterpart. In this regard, the bankers also ensure that there are no vitiating elements like fraud, undue influence, misrepresentation etc that will invalidate a contract entered into by such persons and thereby, they respect his or her autonomy, dignity and privacy.

As per SBI chief legal manager[115] disabled persons including visually impaired along with the senior citizens are given priority over other account holders.

SBI Chief Manager[116] stated that the employment opportunities, loans at concessional rates to support self employment, vocational training for visually impaired are reserved and facilitated as per their circulars and notifications from the RBI, which are again directed for implementation from the State or Central Government Schemes and programmes.

3.2.3 Certifying Authorities

- Karnataka Institute of Medical Science(KIMS) and Government District Hospitals

KIMS has been designated as certifying authority since its inception in the year 1956. Earlier the Head of the department of Opthomology used to certify but later from the year 2006, a three member panel was created consisting of Ophthalmologist, medical specialist and the superintendent of the institute to certify the person as visually impaired. KIMS is currently following the same procedures and guidelines for certifying the visually disabled as is provided in the Disability Act of 1995. Dr. Sunil Gokhale, lecturer in

---

[115]N.S.Parvartikar is the chief legal manager, Administrative Office, Hubballi

[116]Mr. Vishwanath Hegde is the chief manager, human resource.

KIMS, although being aware of the provisions of the new enactment is waiting for the schemes and programmes from the State Government in this regard. The persons designated are specialists in Opthomology. Figure 12 depicts KIMS Hospital.

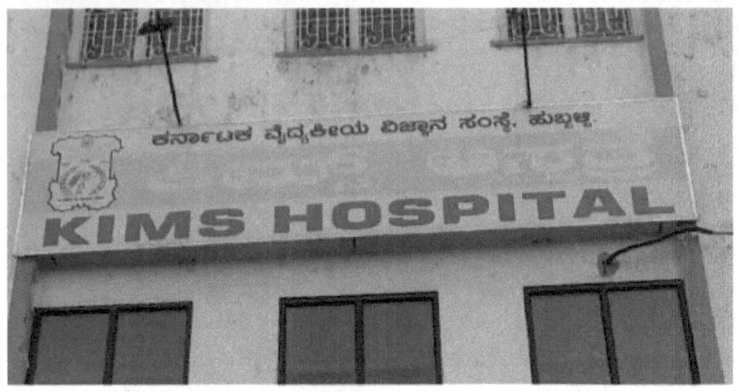

Fig. 13: KIMS Hospital, Hubballi

On an average 10 to 12 patients per month are certified as visually disabled and annually it may extend up to 180 to 200 persons.

Dr. Sunil Gokhale[117] has two concern regarding the certification of visually impaired. One is the blindness of one eye and the second is the colour blindness. Both are not included to be certified as visually disabled and are not even considered for any benefits nor any facilities from the Government.

Dr. Sunil Gokhale, Lecturer, Community Medicine is aware of the new enactment and is updated with all the provisions of the new legislation to acknowledge the changes made to KIMS. He also imparts the changes made in the enactment regarding visually impaired in his lectures along with the

---

[117]Dr. Sunil Gokhale, Lecturer, Community Medicine, KIMs became blind at the age of 23 after his MBBS in KIMS. He got job in KIMS at the age of 35. Currently he is working as Lecturer in Community Medicine Department, KIMS.

causes of such health issues to public and Government institutions concerned with visually impaired persons. He has conducted five lectures on the Act of 2016 till now and also expressed his eagerness to conduct such lectures in Universities in future.

As per the respective Government Departmental orders KIMS conducts free check-up in all schools yearly in the month of August. The full month of August is reserved for such check-ups. Generally, KIMS conducts these free check-ups through appropriate Govt. orders at Non-Government Organizations and at Government Hospital, Old Hubballi, for all city and rural public at large.

KIMS organizes every month free eye check-up in village areas and the patients suffering from cataract are operated free of cost in KIMS department of Opthomology under the supervision of specialists. Around 20 patients are operated per month for the cataract disease. Priority has been given to visually impaired (OPD) patients for their treatment in KIMS. Sexual and reproductive healthcare guidance especially for women with disability is provided at the request of the patient or if felt necessary by the concerned doctors.

KIMS in this year (2018) along with an NGO which is registered in Bangalore named "Saksham" has conducted an event to create awareness in schools regarding the disabilities including visually impaired. Dr. Sunil Gokhale has also undertaken a research on "cross sectional study on health status of visually impaired children of Government blind school, Siddharoodmath, Hubballi" in the year 2002. He also made a research on "eye donation" in the year 2017.

In addition to KIMS, District Hospitals Dharwad also function as certifying authority.[118]

3.2.4 Employment Exchange

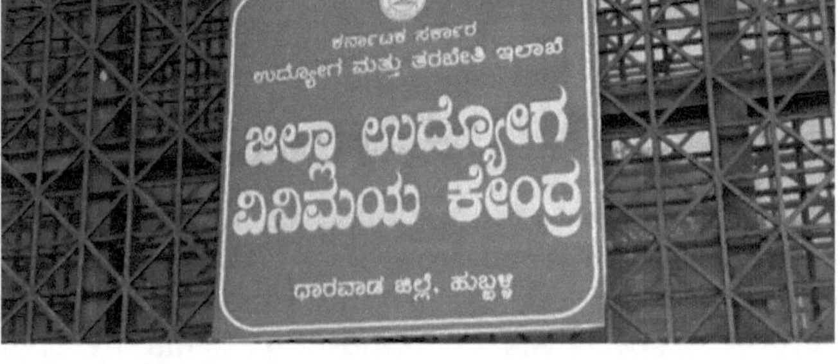

Fig. 14: District Employment Exchange Centre, Hubballi

District Employment Exchange Office, Hubballi makes registration made by persons seeking employment and their renewal after the expiry. The disabled persons are

---

[118]Since 1956 the visually impaired were certified by the District Civil Government hospitals located throughout the State which resulted in lack of clarity as to the exact statistics of persons with disabilities. The position has improved recently and the procedure of certification is in accordance with the 2016 Act wherein, they have demarcated the jurisdiction of government aided medical institutions and district civil hospitals.

allowed for life time registration validity and thereby, are exempted from renewals. They maintain records for persons with disabilities as per the type of disability, gender wise segregating under different categories such as SC/ST, OBC, General, respectively. Thus they maintain all records systematically. The records maintained are reported quarterly with statistics segregating again the disabled persons their category and gender. These records are open to inspection at all reasonable hours by Deputy Director, Joint Director, and State Commissioner, who are all from State level officers from Bangalore.

Although the District Employment Exchange Office is not a Special Employment Exchange office meant for disabled persons as per the Act of 2016[119] but it reports to the Special Employment Exchange office in Bangalore for any educational, training or employment facilities, assistance or guidance provided to persons with disabilities.

The employment exchange office currently has 3 staff members[120] which are:

1. One Assistant Director

2. One First Division Clerk and

3. One second Division Clerk[121]

---

[119]Under Sec. 2(zb) of the RPWD Act, 2016 "Special Employment Exchange" means any office or place established and maintained by the Government for the collection and furnishing of information, either by keeping of registers or otherwise, regarding—

(i) persons who seek to engage employees from amongst the persons with disabilities;

(ii) persons with benchmark disability who seek employment;

(iii) vacancies to which persons with benchmark disabilities seeking employment may be appointed;

[120]One person with orthopedic disability has been employed in one of its ITI wings and there are vacancies to be filled which are open and reserved to visually disabled as well. All these vacancies are to be filled as per Government selection procedures.

[121]In the employment exchange office still four vacant positions are to be filled, namely:

1. Assistant employment officer

2. One second Division Clerk

3. Two group D vacancies.

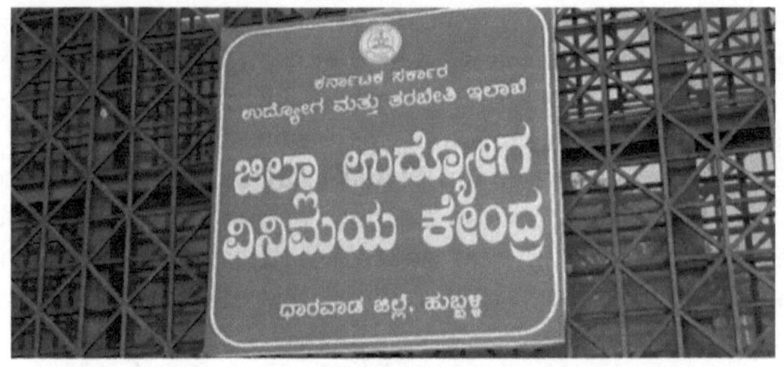

The employment exchange office, Hubballi works in the capacity of Human Resource Development Centre and thereby, provides training for at least two disabled persons who are to be recruited in Govt. sector every year as per the eligibility norms prepared by the Government from time to time. Currently it is also providing training for all the competitive exams such as IAS, KAS, KPSE and others. It also conducts programs on career guidance along with the Government schemes on employment, computer skill development programs and training in English and body language for interviews and communication skills.

Mrs. Sadana Pote[122] in addition to meeting the needs of abled employment seekers in the District, is also aware of State govt. schemes and programmes including provisions of loans at concessional rates to facilitate and support employment of persons with disabilities especially for their vocational training and self-employment. She holds the post of Grievance Redressal Officer along with the position of Assistant Director and does maintain a register of complaints and is aware of the time frame of its resolution along with the time frame provided under right to Information for any queries put before her by the general public at large or by any other organisation.

---

[122]Ms. Sadhana Pote (IAS) is the Asst. Director for District Employment Exchange Office, Navanagar, Hubballi.

Annually the District Exchange Office conducts job fairs for all job seekers in the district including the disabled persons. In addition to this, NGOs also arrange job fares in the premises of Employment Exchange.[123]

Summing Up

The institutions working for the persons with disabilities are scattered in the Hubballi-Dharwad area. Empirical study on these visually disabled in Hubballi-Dharwad area touching upon the Government blind schools, institutions including banks, braille book transcription centers, certifying authorities, employment exchanges and other NGOs working for the blind regarding their extent of awareness as to the newly adopted legislation of 2016 reflects a grim situation. When it comes to education, both primary and secondary, most of the institutions including the schools are not having sufficient staffs and most of the vacancies remain unfilled for years together. The study has also exposed to the shocking revelation that in some of the institutions the positions filled are not as per the eligibility criteria. The blind children are devoid of even proper infrastructure facilities including proper food, hygine, ramps, mobility teachers in their staff and above all there is lack of security for the blind girl children. The parents have expressed their insecurity for their children, both boys and girls, in the residential schools in the wake of increasing sexual offences against children in these days. When it comes to higher education and employment opportunities, to secure the future of these children in spite of the joint efforts of employment exchanges, NGOs for their higher education and employment the new enactment takes

---

[123]Recently a non-government organization named Association of people with disability from Belgaum had conducted a job fair for persons with disablities in Hubli and Dharwad area, in which it has placed six persons with disabilities and selected 46 for training under it for preparing them for the respective jobs.

a long way in its implementation. The Sahana Charitable Trust for Braille Book Transcription Centre in North Karnataka has approached many administrative officers and ministers regarding their willingness to provide free braille text books to the visually impaired in the State for their higher studies which was promised to be looked into but is still pending for consideration. To mention the initiative of the National Federation of Blind, various law courts have given land mark decisions in order to recognize protect and promote entitlements of persons with disabilities. Despite the lack of co-operation among the government most of the institutions and NGO's are ready to provide much support and assistance to the governmental departments in their own fields of expertise but here also they are not yet approached and consulted. If consulted it would have resolved the time constraint in the implementation of the new Act. In matters of employment also although there is a District employment exchange office it is essential to have a special employment exchange office for disabled in the district which will reduce the time and other difficulties of the disabled. Even most of the governmental departments and institutions for disabled persons including the certifying authorities are invoking the provisions of the repealed PWD Act of 1995 for their administrative functions. For the welfare of lakhs of persons with disabilities in the State who are still waiting for the assistance of government there should be effective implementation of the 2016 legislation which should reach them at the earliest which they do not claim as sympathy but rather as a right …..

CHAPTER 4

INCLUSIVE EDUCATIONAL MEASURES AS A REMEDY

According to 2011 census there are 2,68,10,557 blind persons in the India in which most of them belong to the under privileged strata of the society. Blindness combined with poverty limits their access to education, employment, health services, etc. which finally leads to their socio-economic exclusion. The census provides that 45% of India's disabled population are still illiterate compared to 26% of all Indians. Sarva Shiksha Abhiyan, the national educational initiative to help realise universal elementary education policy aims:

Every child with special needs should be placed in regular schools with the needed support services.

However, the ground realities of the disabled population are totally different. Among the government's initiative to provide free education for all children between 6 and 14[124] those with special needs form the largest out-of-school group in the country. The dropout rates of disabled children are very high. Of the persons with disabilities who are educated only 59% complete class X compared to 67% of the general population.[125] When it comes to Karnataka State among 2.84 lakhs visually impaired persons only 10,000 are getting education[126] and the education facilities and other assistance provided by the State is limited only up to Xth

---

[124]This is stated as per the 86th Constitution Amendment Act which through Art. 21 A of the Constitution.

[125]Hindustan Times, Why 45% of India's disabled are still illiterate and thousands dropping out of schools.

[126]Nijaguni Dhindala Koppa, Blind's educational life lightened by Braille system, Vijaya Karnataka Newspaper, 30th June, 2018, Hubballi. This statistics is as per the estimated 6% growth rate calculated from the 2011 Census.

standard. However, in Hubballi-Dharwad area among the total population of 943788 persons the exact population of visually impaired is not properly maintained as the certifying authorities are designated to certify from other districts as well. As of now, there is no certainty as to the exact figures of the visually impaired.[127] Most of the schools in Karnataka are providing education for the children with disabilities in special schools. When the Ministry of Human Resource Development propagates an inclusive education model where special children study in regular classrooms the Ministry of Social Justice and Empowerment express confidence for separate schools for children with special needs. The idea of integrating these children with special needs with the non disabled is far from imagination in small Cities like Hubballi- Dharwad. In this way, the ethos of the Convention on disability regarding inclusive education has not been fulfilled in its true sense. An attempt is made in this regard to understand the meaning of inclusive education and its evolution.

4.1 Meaning and evolution of Inclusive Education:

During present times the normal trend in providing education for children with disabilities has been to focus on their education in the same setting as their peer groups without special needs. The education that is strongly advocated for children with disabilities is inclusive education. The term 'inclusion' refers to attending the same school as the pupil would have attended in the absence of a significant special need.[128] It implies a radical shift from segregation, a radical reform of school in terms of curriculum, assessment, pedagogy and grouping of pupils.

In brief, what inclusion means for children with disabilities is:

[127]Recently, the State Government has announced to have census for the disabled.
[128]Prakash, Jayanti (2005), "Inclusive education: voices from the other side". *I.J.D.S*, 1(1):92-113.

(a)   Educating children with disabilities and those without in the same schools

(b)   Providing services, support and advice for parents of all children in regular settings

(c)   Training and supporting regular education teachers and administers

(d)   Children with disabilities to follow the same schedules as other children

(e)   Encouraging friendships and mutual respect between all children with and without disabilities

(f)   Teaching all children to understand and accept differences, be it race, colour, sex, ethnicity, language, nationality, social origin, religion, disability, poverty, birth or other status.[129]

Analysing the evolution of the concept of inclusive education till it found place in the International Convention on Disability it is to be noted that the concept has developed over years. The concept of inclusive education has been put on the agenda and propelled forward by the Disabled Peoples Organizations (DPOs). DPOs achieved this agenda through organized political pressure and mobilizing allies. As a result, progress towards inclusive education though slow has been steady over the last twenty-five years. A historical analysis of international documents gives clear evidence of this conceptual shift in thinking. While the UN Declaration on the Rights of Disabled Persons, 1975[130] focused on assisting the disabled individual to develop activities, capabilities, and self-reliance for functioning in normal life, the Dakar Final Report on Education for All Progress since Jomtein[131] 2000

---

[129]Habibi, Gulbadan (1999), "UNICEF and Children with Disabilities", *Education Update*, 2(4):7-33.

[130]By Resolution 3447(xxx) of 9 December 1975, the General Assembly proclaimed the Declaration on the Rights of Disabled Persons. See United Nations (1994), United Nations in the field of Human Rights, New York.

[131]The World Education Forum, held in Dakar from 26 to 28 April 2000 was the culminating event of the decade of Education for All (EFA) initiated in Jomtien, Thailand in 1990.

pointed out that instead of focusing on preparing children to fit into existing schools, the new emphasis focuses on preparing schools so that they can deliberately reach out to all children.[132]

Since 1999, momentum for disability rights has grown exponentially. In 2001, the UN Commission on Human Rights passed resolution 2000/51 on Human Rights of People with Disabilities. The Commission set out a number of specific procedures whereby, States must improve the rights of disabled people including their right to inclusive education.[133]

Besides these movements, several world congresses have also passed resolutions, and declarations, with relevance to inclusive education. These include:

- Salamanca Declaration and Framework for Action (1994)
- Beijing Declaration on Rights of People with Disabilities in the New Century (2000)[134]
- Declaration of the World Assembly in Sapporo (2002)[135]
- Declaration of Biwako (2002)
- G-8 Summit to Inclusion (2002)[136]
- European Year of Disabled Persons (2003) [137]
- Kochi Declaration (2003)[138]

---

[132]UNESCO (2002), World Education Forum Final Report, Part II: Improving the quality and equity of education for all. Sub section entitled "Meeting special and diverse education needs: making inclusive education a reality".

133Resolutions are available at www.unhchr.ch

[134]Beijing Declaration adopted on 12 March 2000 at the World NGO Summit on Disability. Beijing, People's Republic of China, available at URL: http://www.rehab-international.org/aboutri/beijingdeclaration.html

[135]Sapporo Declaration, October 2002, available at http://www.dpi-japan.org/8wa/declaration2002e.html

[136]G-8 Summit to Inclusion (2002), available at http://www.g7.utoronto.ca/evaluations/2002kananaskis/assessment_africaplan.html

[137]European Year of Disabled Persons(2003), available at http://www.edf-feph.org/en/events/year/year.htm

[138]Kochi Declaration (2003), Kochi, Kerala, India; available at http://www.inclusion-international.org/site_uploads/1119008867197086195.pdf

Several of these declarations have brought to the attention of the United Nations the need to constitute a special Convention on the rights of disabled people[139] which ultimately resulted in the Convention on disability. Thus inclusive education has found a legal basis under international law in 2006 through the adoption of the Convention on the Rights of Persons with Disabilities (CRPD). This has resulted in a further boost to the promotion of inclusive education around the world. Nonetheless, it remains to be seen whether these developments have had any favourable influence. Although the CRPD has been ratified in many countries and welcomed by international organisations, changes are not happening on the ground and discussions often appear to lead nowhere.[140]

Recommendations to send children with disabilities to mainstream schools were first made in the Sargent Report in 1944 and again in 1964 by the Kothari Commission.[141] Despite this, the change has been slow with segregation in special schools dominating the scene until recently. The 1995 Persons with Disabilities Act stated that disabled children should be educated in integrated settings where possible, however, as understood, it was mainly the lacuna in the implementation which was one of the factors that made the Act to be reincarnated as the Rights of Persons with Disabilities Act,

---

[139]The International Disability Alliance(IDA), a consortium of international DPOs (Disabled People's International, Inclusion International, Rehabilitation International, World Federation of the Deaf, World Federation of the Deaf-Blind, World Network of Users and Survivors of Psychiatry) even passed a resolution outlining critical points pertaining the proposed Convention Peters, Susan J (2003), "Inclusive education: Achieving education for all by including those with Disabilities and Special education needs", [Online: web] Accessed 6 September 2016

URL:http://siteresources.worldbank.org/DISABILITY/Resources/280658-1172610312075/ InclusiveEduPeters.pdf

[140]Moore and Slee, R. Disability Studies, Education and Exclusion in N. Watson, A. Roulstone and C. Thomas (eds) Routledge *Handbook of Disability Studies*, (London: Routledge, 2012) 225-239

[141]Shalini Yadava, "Inclusive Education: Challenges and Prospects in India", *Educationia Confab*, Vol.2, No.4 (2013)

2016. An attempt is made to analyze the concept of inclusive education in the light of evolution of the Convention on the Rights of Persons with Disabilities

4.1.1 Inclusive Education under the Convention

The CRPD is the first internationally binding legal treaty on disability rights exclusively and globally representing a paradigm shift from a medical and charitable model to a social model embracing the rights of people with disabilities to be included in the community enabling them to be independent citizens. The Convention has thus recast disability as a social construction[142] and thereby, has brought a human rights dimension to disability issues. The fifty articles of the treaty cover issues from education to employment and respect for the home and family, all with the general focus of non-discrimination and equality of treatment.[143] The very first article spells out the purpose of the 50-article Convention, i.e. "to promote, protect and ensure the full enjoyment of all human rights and fundamental freedoms by all persons with disabilities and also to promote respect for their inherent dignity". The Convention does not prohibit discrimination on the ground of disability alone but covers the whole spectrum of civil, political, economic, cultural and social rights. Article 8 the Convention mandates State parties to take effective and appropriate measures to create awareness throughout society regarding rights of persons with disabilities and foster respect for their rights and dignity. For this, the Convention advises State parties to initiate and maintain public awareness campaigns. Article 12 requires State parties to recognize that persons with disabilities enjoy legal capacity on an equal basis with others

---

[142]The convention takes the view that disability stems from the failure of social environment to meet the needs and aspirations of persons with disabilities.

[143]See Convention on the Rights of Persons with Disabilities (CRPD), Dec. 6, 2006, *available at* http://www.un.org/disabilities/convention/conventionfull.shtml (last visited August 23, 2018).

in all aspects of life.

Right to education is provided under Art 24 of the Convention which should be read and analyzed in conjunction with other rights provided in the Convention and also in the light of general principles of the Convention enunciated in Article 3. General Principles postulated in Article 3 of the Convention are (a) respect for inherent dignity, (b) non-discrimination, (c) full and effective participation and inclusion in society, (d) respect for difference and acceptance of disability as part of human diversity and humanity, (e) equality of opportunity, (f) accessibility, (g) equality between men and women, (h) respect for the evolving capacities of children with disabilities and respect for the rights of children with disabilities to preserve their identities. Thus the overall obligation to be achieved under Article 24 is the realization of an inclusive education system at all levels. Although the Convention is the first legally binding instrument to introduce the concept of inclusive education in the midst of soft laws already discussed in the preceding section it has failed to define inclusive education. This lacuna however, has been taken care by the CRPD Committee as viewing inclusive education as:

a dynamic approach of responding positively to pupil diversity and of seeing individual differences not as problems, but as opportunities for enriching learning[144]

The Committee has conceptualized inclusive education as a:

(a) fundamental human right of all children thereby, subordinating parental responsibilities to the rights of the children

---

[144]This view has already been advanced by UNESCO. See UNESCO (2005), Guidelines for Inclusion: Ensuring Access to Education for All. Available online: http://unesdoc.unesco. org/images/0014/001402/ 140224e.pdf (accessed on 20 October 2017).

(b) fundamental principle that values the well-being, inherent dignity, autonomy of all students thereby, recognizing the ability to be included in the society.

(c) primary means of realizing other human rights

(d) continuing commitment to eliminate all the barriers in right to education

In its General Comment No 4, the CRPD Committee also traced the boundaries among the prevailing barriers like exclusion, segregation, discrimination etc., with a view to overcome the same and to help them to participate in the mainstream education system creating a feeling of oneness and thereby, helping them in fulfilling the obligations incorporated in Art. 24 of the Convention.[145] Most interestingly, Article 24 para 3 (c) makes specific allowance for some separate provision for children who are blind, deaf or deaf blind. The relevant obligation is to ensure that their education is 'delivered in the most appropriate languages and modes and means of communication for the individual and in environments which maximize academic and social development'. In this regard Gerard Quinn, a leading authority on international and comparative disability law and policy points that it is a very interesting way of squaring separate provision with the overall goal of inclusion and also hints a caution of warning that it is the tightly cabined exception that proves the rule and the new monitoring body will have to take care to ensure that it does not undermine the thrust of mainstreaming.[146]

---

[145]CRPD Committee. (2016). General Comment No 4 Article 24: Right to Inclusive Education (Adopted 26 August 2016). Available online: http://www.ohchr.org/EN/HRBodies/CRPD/Pages/GC.aspx (accessed on 20 September 2018).

[146]Gerard Quinn, "A Short Guide to the United Nations Convention on the Rights of Persons with Disabilities", *1 Eur. Y.B. Disability L. 89 (2009)*

4.1.2 Inclusive Education under Indian Scenario

Inclusive education that demands persons with disabilities not to be excluded from the general education system 'on the basis of disability' has always faced difficulties in its implementation may it be the PWD Act, 1995 that failed to protect the rights of persons with disabilities or the newly adopted legislation on disability. Analysis of the PWD Act, 1995 had emphasized on dual approach on education where they promoted inclusive education emphasizing at the same time the role of special schools. Even after the 1995 Act was repealed various concerns on inclusive education have been raised regarding the underlying principles and its implementation.

The term 'inclusive education' was included in the Five Year Plan (2005-2012) under 'inclusive growth' as its focus. Ministry of Human Resource and Development during this period of plan developed the Action Plan for Inclusive Education of Children and Youth with Disabilities, 2005 which resulted in various criticisms from disability organizations. In 2006, Ministry of Social Justice and Empowerment developed the National Policy for Persons with Disabilities which emphasized the need for mainstreaming of the persons with disabilities in the general education system through inclusive education and at the same time expressed confidence for special schools for children with special needs. The scheme of Inclusive Education for Disabled at Secondary Stage (IEDSS) has been launched from the year 2009-10. This scheme replaces the earlier scheme of Integrated Education for Disabled Children (IEDC) and provides assistance for inclusive education for disabled children in classes IX-XII. This scheme is now subsumed under Rashtriya Madhyamik Shiksha Abhiyan (RMSA) from 2013.

The Rights of Persons with Disabilities Act, 2016 is enacted in consonance with the International Convention on Disability and intents to implement inclusive education at all levels. Analysing some provisions which directly or indirectly specify inclusive education include Sec. 2 (m) of the Act which defines inclusive education as:

a system of education wherein students with and without disability learn together and the system of teaching and learning is suitably adapted to meet the learning needs of different types of students with disabilities

The duties of educational institutions and specific measures to promote and facilitate inclusive education are provided in Sections 16 and 17 of the Act along with the measures to promote, protect and ensure participation of persons with disabilities in adult education and continuing education programmes equally with others.

Accordingly, Sec. 16 of the Rights of Persons with Disabilities Act, 2016[147] mandates the appropriate Governments and the local authorities to endeavor that all educational institutions funded or recognised by them provide inclusive education to the children with disabilities with the goal of full inclusion. It also imposes a duty to ensure that education to children who are blind should be imparted in the most appropriate languages and modes and means of communication. With a view to achieve the above objectives the Act further provides that appropriate governments should take adequate measures to (i) conduct survey of school going children in every five years for identifying children with disabilities for ascertaining their special needs.[148] (ii) establish adequate number of teacher training institutions (iii) train and employ teachers, including teachers with disability who are qualified

---

[147]Art. 16 in addition provides for attaining a barrier free environment without discrimination including transportation facilities to the children

[148]The Act specifies conducting of first survey within a period of two years from the commencement of the Act.

in sign language and braille and also teachers who are trained in teaching children with intellectual disability (iv) train professionals and staff to support inclusive education at all levels of school education (v) promote the use of braille and sign language to supplement the use of one's own speech to fulfill the daily communication needs of persons with speech, communication or language disabilities and enables them to participate and contribute to the society (vi) provide books, other learning materials and appropriate assistive devices to students with benchmark disabilities free of cost up to the age of eighteen years (vii) provide scholarships in appropriate cases to students with benchmark disability (viii) make suitable modifications in the curriculum and examination system to meet the needs of students with disabilities such as extra time for completion of examination paper, facility of scribe or amanuensis, exemption from second and third language courses.

The Act drafted in consonance with the International Convention further lays focus on the prevention of those diseases which causes disabilities and also focuses on awareness campaigns and rehabilitation measures of persons with disabilities which implies many steps on the part of the government for its implementation.

4.2 Institutional views on Inclusive education in Hubballi-Dharwad Area

Inclusive education in the State of Karnataka has been gathered from the institutional views of a group of residential schools, educational institutions and Universities which are enumerated below.

4.2.1 Government Educational Instituions

- Shri Aroodha education society's Residential School for blind children

The residential educational society has an open view on inclusive education and has expressed their willness and views towards inclusive education. In their view the main hindrance is in the absence of mobility trainers which is a must for the disabled children including visually impaired children in normal educational institutions which ultimately hampers the educational capabilities and reduces the motivation and encouragement of blind children. If mobility trainers are also made part of the faculty of the normal educational institute than there can be a transition towards inclusive education. If special trainers are also the part of the faculty as per the planned curriculum for both the normal and visually impaired children it should not hamper the time frame of completing the syllabus for both the students. Since the learning and understanding capabilities of both the children varies as per their physical abnormalities the education is preferred to be only sole special educational and residential institutes particularly for the visually impaired children.

Currently almost all the special blind schools are residential in nature wherein, they are provided with all the residential facilities with accommodation. This again in turn will benefit the visually impaired in reducing their strain and trouble of travelling from their own residence to the educational institutes. If all the required residential facilities along with the accommodation is provided in these inclusive educational institutions for visually impaired children then inclusive education can be beneficial to them.

As the blind children will have difficulties in coping with their counterpart in their inability to grasp with ease in specific subjects like mathematics, statistics, yoga etc., it will be feasible if the same system of opting the subjects as per their capabilities is provided. It will again be an added advantage if the blind children are provided with devices such as braille literature, musical instruments, craft, computer and technological appliances such as JAWS, audio recordings, etc. to supplement their optional subjects.

It is also expected that in case the inclusive education is implemented in small cities like Hubballi-Dharwad there are more chances wherein, these children will be discriminated and isolated by their own classmates themselves. The parents of normal children may also show their reluctance to educate their children with the disabled and may ultimately not favour the concept of inclusive education itself. The attitude, maturity levels of the children also plays a dominant role in its success. But the maturity is expected from the children to be attained at their college level and not in their schooling age. If the number of visually impaired students is less in number as compared to the normal students the confidence of those visually impaired students gradually reduces and the interest of the teachers are also diverted subjecting the children to discrimination.

- Government Residential School for Blind Boys, Siddharoodmath

Siddharood Blind Boys Government School through the senior teachers and parents expressed the advantages of inclusive education by pointing that it facilitates education to all children with special needs at their own native places in the normal schools located nearby their residence and provides education along with their siblings and neighbours creating homely atmosphere in their education. In their views it provides safe, secured way of procuring education to their children with special needs and to the satisfaction of their parents and guardians. Again, currently there is lack of transportation and communication facilities for these children there is immense increase in the percentage of absentees which in turn, increases the gaps in their school education but with the introduction of inclusive education this problem will be eliminated.

The teachers also anticipated the negative impact in the implementation of inclusive education as there are more chances of increase in the percentage of special children in discontinuing their education due to immediate introduction.

Currently the normal teachers are made to handle the Children with Special Needs (CWSN) in the existing special schools due to negligence in filling the required vacancies, so there is unanimous suggestion among teachers to recruit suitable number of special trained teachers in normal schools if the inclusive education is to be successfully implemented. In this prevailing situation if inclusive education is introduced, there are more chances that the children may not be evaluated specially and properly and may be simply made to attend the classrooms providing them with pass certificates to pursue further studies which further hinders their flow of learning process compared to the special schools which use to provide special care and attention to them. Although, the senior most teacher of the school is totally against the inclusive education specifically for the blind and the mentally retarded persons, they had at the same time few suggestions for its effective implementation. The teachers suggested that there should be systematic training for them along with one optional special course for any particular disability in their regular B.Ed/D.Ed courses. This allows the teacher to plan their teaching pattern and be facilitated and acquainted with the required materials and devices for imparting their knowledge and skills. In the wake of these disturbing circumstances the pertinent question to be answered is that when there is a need for special atmosphere, infrastructure and facilities to be provided for the CWSN in the existing special schools, whether the same will be provided in the normal schools for the CWSN.

After Analysing the prevailing situations in school level

mainly, pre-primary, primary and secondary education an attempt is also made in the context of inclusive education depicting the current situation already in existence in two major Universities situated in the heart of Hubballi-Dharwad.

- Karnatak University, Dharwad (KUD):

Fig. 15: Karnatak University, Dharwad

Karnatak University has been implementing the State Government schemes as per the notifications and circulars issued from time to time in matters pertaining to inclusive education. The University is complying with the requirements of reservation of seats for persons with disabilities as per Section 32(1) and (2) of the RPWD Act, 2016 which is not less than five percent and is also providing an upper age relaxation of five years for their admission in institutions of higher education. The list of the students with disabilities registered for the Under Graduation and Post Graduation Courses in the Dharwad District and also in the affiliated colleges under KUD, Dharwad for the Post Graduation courses in the year 2016 – 2017 and 2017 – 2018 is provided in Tables 6 and 7:[149]

Number of persons with disabilities registered for the Under Graduate and Post Graduate Courses in the

[149]The information is collected from Bhimrai Mundaragi, Assistant Office Superintendent, University Information Cell, KUD, Dharwad.

Dharwad District in affiliated colleges:

Table 6: No. of persons with disabilities registered for the Under Graduate and Post Graduate Courses in the affiliated colleges

Under Graduate Courses				Post Graduate Courses			
2016 – 2017		2017 – 2018		2016 – 2017		2017 – 2018	
Male	83	Male	74	Male	00	Male	03
Female	56	Female	39	Female	00	Female	00
Total	139	Total	113	Total	00	Total	03

Source : Primary data

Number of disabled registered for the Post Graduate Courses in the Dharwad University Campus:

Table 7: No. of persons with disabilities registered in Dharwad University Campus

2016 – 2017		2017 – 2018	
Male	07	Male	30
Female	12	Female	16
Total	19	Total	46

Source : Primary data

The Superintendent, Confidential Section (Evaluation)[150] stated that since three years Karnatak University has been

[150]Mr. Korishettar is the Superintendent, Confidential Section (Evaluation) of KUD

allowing their respective affiliated colleges and educational institutions to verify and scrutinize on their own the scribe applications and has disbursed all the required forms to be filled and submitted by such applicants to the respective college and educational institutions. The University Squad and supervisors are assisted by the institutions at the time of examinations. Hence the University has not maintained any records relating to the number of visually impaired appearing and completing the under graduation and post graduation courses from the University through these institutions.

In the Doctorate level studies[151], the senior assistant, PhD department informed that only two disabled (one low vision and another with one eye impaired) have enrolled in the current year 2018 – 2019 from Arts and Management department respectively and there are no other enrolment of visually impaired in the Science and Social Science Department.

Though Karnatak University encourages the integrated and inclusive education system and has also provided all the facilities required as per the new legislation for inclusive education, as of now, there is less response from the educational institutions regarding the facilities to be provided and there is less awareness even in the society.

- Karnataka State Law University, Hubballi (KSLU):

Fig. 16: Karnataka State Law University, Hubballi

[151]Mrs. Ashwini S. O. is the senior assistant PhD department of KUD

Karnataka State Law University, the only State Law University with 106 affiliated colleges throughout the State under it is aware of the five percent reservation of seats for PWD in admissions of students and revealed that the number of PWD students getting themselves enrolled to the University and affiliated colleges are less than two percent. The Administration and Academic section of KSLU[152] provided the information that there are dropouts and discontinued students even among the normal students due to the vast syllabus to pass the exam and as there is no exemption from PWD to join and complete the law courses with ease. These streams of students many a times find themselves over-burdened. Presently in law courses the students with disabilities are not provided any subject relaxations and exemption when compared to other degree courses like B.Com and B.Sc.[153] In matters relating to the upper age limit relaxation of five years for PWD is still controversial and is pending in the courts for final decision. Currently KSLU is admitting students irrespective of their age limit for pursuing their courses with a prior undertaking signed by the students to adhere to the decisions of the court prior to the completion of their courses.

The statistics of the students enrolled in the university campus provided the lowest strength of PWD against the reservation provided to them. The list of those enrolled for both the graduation and master's courses in law for the academic year 2016 – 2017 and 2017 – 2018 in the University is provided in Table: 8

---

[152]Mr. Sunil Saptasagar is one of the case workers in the Administrative and Academic section of KSLU

[153]In B.Sc and B.Com there are optional subjects provided for disabled in subjects like Mathematics and Chemistry wherein, the students can opt for music and Singing.

Table 8: Total disabled students enrolled in the University campus for the academic year 2016-18.

Five Years LL.B (B.A./ B.B.A. / B.Com. Integrated Honor's LL.B.)				One Year LL.M			
2016 – 2017		2017 – 2018		2016 – 2017		2017 – 2018	
Male	00	Male	00	Male	00	Male	00
Female	01	Female	01	Female	00	Female	01
Total	01	Total	0	Total	00	Total	01

Source : Primary data

The overall strength of visually impaired in Karnataka State colleges affiliated to KSLU for past two academic years is shown in Table : 9

Table 9 : Persons with disabilities affiliated to KSLU in 2016-17 and 2017-2018

Three Years LL.B				Five Years LL.B (B.A / B.B.A / B.Com. Integrated LL.B)			
2016 – 2017		2017 – 2018		2016 – 2017		2017 – 2018	
Male	01	Male	01	Male	01	Male	-
Female	01	Female	-	Female	01	Female	-
Total	02	Total	01	Total	02	Total	Nil

Source : Primary data

The overall strength of visually impaired in Dharwad District colleges affiliated to KSLU for past two academic years i.e. for 2016 – 2017 and 2017 – 2018 for Three Years LL.B and Five Years LL.B (B.A./ B.B.A./ B.Com. Integrated LL.B) is nil

4.2.2 Distant Educational Institutions:

- Institute of Company Secretaries of India (ICSI), Institute of Cost and Management Accountants of India (ICMAI) and Institute of Chartered Accountants of India (ICAI)

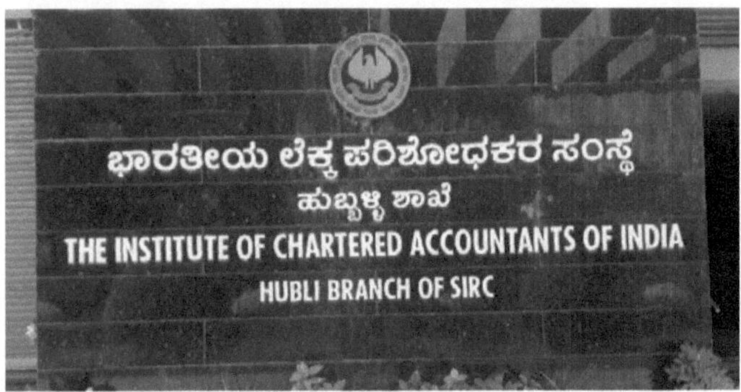

Fig. 17: The Institute of Chartered Accountants of India, Hubballi

Institute of Company Secretaries of India, Institute of Cost and Management Accountants of India[154] and Institute of Chartered Accountants of India, Keshwapur, Hubballi Branch, have expressed their concern about the non availability of data pertaining to the number of disabled in the Dharwad District as the registration and admission process has been made through online and the data can only be procured through its registered head office located at Delhi and Chennai respectively. The study centre even run coaching classes on behalf of the Institute but have not

[154]Study Centre and Examination centre of ICSI and ICMA is in 'Jnana Degula' near K.M.F., Dharwad

yet come across any student with visual disability having enrolled in their coaching classes. What could be inferred is that as these courses are competitive in nature it could be the difficulty in getting through the exams along with procuring the required aggregate marks in all the subjects at a time that prevents the visually disabled students from getting enrolled in such competitive courses.

Fig. 18: The Institute of Company Secretaries of India Study Centre, Dharwad

- Indira Gandhi National Open University (IGNOU)

Fig. 19 Indira Gandhi National Open University, Dharwad Study Centre, Dharwad

Dharwad is the study centre for IGNOU. As the courses are offered through on-line and only week end classes are conducted, attendance is not compulsory. Therefore, there is no much scope for inclusive education.[155] The centre conducts examination in its study centre building and if any such visually impaired students are enrolled, the scribe applications are verified at the Vijayapura Regional Circle office as per the application submitted in Dharwad office for its eligibility requirements and the Dharwad office is required to assist the supervisors and squad members in the examination.

4.2.3   Other Private Educational Institutions

- Dr. D.G. Shetty Educational Society, Dharwad[156]

The Society runs Pre-University, Degree colleges and Post Graduation Courses in Gyana Degula, Dharwad. Although, they are neither against nor in favour of implementing inclusive education in their institute, they have shown their eagerness in implementation when proper support and co-operation from the respective departments and its officials are provided. The society states that it has not came across any student with visual disability approaching for his/her enrollment in the college till today. But if approached in future the society has expressed that they will take due care to assist any student in a convenient manner in pursuing their education with high priority along with the other normal children.

---

[155]Mr. Suraj Jain is the Coordinator for IGNOU, Dharwad.

[156]D.G. Shetty Educational Society is running the pre-university, Degree courses in the field of arts, science and commerce stream and masters in commerce post-graduation courses

Fig. 20: Dr. D.G. Shetty Educational Society, Dharwad

J.S.S Educational Institutions:

- J.S.S. Shri Manjunatheshwara Central School, Dharwad

The Principal of the school remembered one visually impaired boy who had completed his matriculation from the school four years back.[157] The boy was admitted in the 6th standard along with other normal students and had no difficulties in pursuing his studies. In spite of the father himself being visually impaired, with his sole support the child could overcome the difficulties in communicating with the staff and all matters that came in his way. This was in spite of the fact that there were neither mobility teachers nor any special teacher for the disabled boy. Even the co-students and the staff had assisted the boy in every way they could and also the normal children learnt how to take care of people with such disabilities. The Principal further expressed that even without any special facilities the boy had completed his 10th class by securing around 88 per centage and therefore, education in the inclusive setting is a positive sign to benefit both the disabled and abled children.

---

[157]Smt. Sadhana S. is the present Principal of the School.

Fig. 21: J.S.S Shri Manjunatheshwara Central School, Dharwad

- J.S.S. R.S. Hukkerikar Arts, Commerce and Science Pre-University College, Vidyagiri Dharwad

Fig. 22: J.S.S. R.S. Hukkerikar Arts, Commerce and Science Pre-University College, Vidyagiri Dharwad

The Principal of the college stated that there are eleven visually impaired students admitted in their 1st and 2nd P.U. College for the year 2018 – 2019.[158] The management had provided fee concessions, free uniforms and permission to use the technical devices such as laptops, audio recording tapes etc. on prior permission and has also provided the proper seating arrangements along with the scribe facilities

---

[158]Mrs. Bharathi V. Shanbagh is the Principal of J.S.S. Pre-University College

in the exams and tests they conduct on frequent intervals of time. The Principal gave the data of students with visual disability who are enrolled in the last 3 academic years for I and II P.U. Classes which are as listed in Table: 10.

Table 10: List of visually disabled enrolled during 2016-19

Year	I P.U.C.			II P.U.C.			Grand Total
	Boys	Girls	Total	Boys	Girls	Total	
2016 – 17	3	1	4	0	3	3	7
2017 – 18	1	1	2	3	0	3	5
2018 – 19	3	2	5	1	0	1	6
	7	4	11	4	3	7	18

Source : Primary data

The students are admitted in Arts section only as per their choice till now and there are no visually disabled students in Commerce and Science sections. The Principal did not find any difficulty in the system of inclusive education in their institute due to the support from the normal students and the staff providing the disabled children with all required assistance with empathy. However, the Principal has concern over the braille books which are not available to the visually impaired at their regular curriculum but are provided only at the end of the course completion and the students fail to complete their studies without the braille books. Almost all the visually disabled students are residing in the Samarthanam Trust.[159] Thus except the non availability of braille books which is a severe hindrance for the children

[159]Samarthanam Trust is an NGO for disabled situated nearby which provides all the other required residential facilities to these visually impaired students.

the support and cooperation of the co-students and staff in the inclusive education system can definitely bring a positive attitude among these children and thereby, find their own identity in the society.

- J.S.S. Banashankari Arts, Commerce and S.K. Gubbi Science Degree College, Dharwad

The visually impaired students after completing their pre-university studies from J.S.S. R.S. Hukkerikar Arts, Commerce and Science Pre-University College enroll themselves for their degree courses in J.S.S. Banashankari Arts, Commerce and S.K. Gubbi Science Degree College in the same campus.[160] As intimated by the staff there are only 3 visually impaired students in their B.A. 5th semester (3rd year) and there are no admissions in the 1st and 2nd year classes. They are of the view that the students either discontinue their studies or continue in gaps as per their convenience or depending upon their backlog subjects.

4.2.4   Employment Exchange training centre

Asst. Director for District Employment Exchange Office, Navanagar, Hubballi is in favour of inclusive education and has accordingly arranged the employment exchange training and career guidance cell meeting the convenience and facilities in terms of its structure and design, not only to the non-disabled but also the differently abled's comfort. The classroom chairs are designed as per the physically and visually challenged persons requirements, the computer and communication classes are user friendly and special care is provided to both physically and visually challenged candidates.

---

[160]Currently G. Krishnamurthy is the Principal of the college.

4.2.5 Non-Governmental Organisations:

- Samarthanam trust for the Disabled, Dharwad

As mentioned in the earlier chapter Samarthanam trust for the Disabled has been putting its efforts in getting the visually impaired to pursue their higher education. It has approached many educational institutes for the admission of visually impaired in pursuing their further studies after schooling. J.S.S. Vidyagiri, Dharwad, K.C.D. Mahanth College and other few institutes have been tied up with the trust in order to get the disabled students continue their further studies with the non-disabled peers. These institutes have managed to encourage and get these disabled students enrolled in their institutes wherein, the trust has also managed to provide facilities and accommodation.

- Chikenkoppad Shree Chennaveer Sharanara's Welfare Ashram for Blind, Hubballi Chikenkoppad has also been providing the same zeal of trust and motivation to many educational institutes in getting their beneficiaries better education in these institutions with overall financial support.

- NAB

NAB promotes visually impaired children to attend normal schools and enable them to interact with the open society from an early stage. NAB has allocated teachers wherein, each teacher is responsible for 8 children to make regular visits to the mainstream schools and educate them along with their able bodied peers with the supply of learning aids for these visually impaired children. The teachers are also responsible to counsel the parents to integrate their children into a normal school and the school authorities to admit visually handicapped children into their mainstream school.

Summing Up

The concept of inclusive education still needs further clarification and even the question as to whether it actually helps the inclusion of children with disabilities in the mainstream is again doubtful. This question poses more doubt equally in international level and national level. Although the CRPD has been ratified by many States and welcomed by international organisations, changes are not happening on the ground and discussions often appear to lead nowhere. While States parties to the Convention have sometimes adopted national legislation that mandates the participation of disabled children in the general education system, measures that would enforce it do not appear to exist. Despite the CRPD's high level of ratification, evidence indicates that disabled children do not get the individual support they need and remain largely unaccepted in regular schools. The situation remains the same even in the case of small cities like Hubbalii- Dharwad. Although the teachers and parents have understood the pros and cons of this concept its implementation requires an effective planning taking into consideration even the minute aspects like adequate infrastructure, staff etc. In the midst of these developments there is much opposition on the implementation of the right to inclusive education.[160] No doubt the Act, if implemented taking adequate measure to overcome the difficulties will be accepted by the disabled community and will be a positive step towards recognizing their rights without any discrimination among those without disability. Above all, it is to be noted that economic, social and cultural rights take on a sharp edge in the context of disability. These cluster of rights that include right to education (Article 24), the right to work (Article 27), the

---

[160]Gauthier De Beco, The right to inclusive education: why is there so much opposition to its implementation?, *International Journal of Law in Context*, 143 (3), 2018 pp 396-415

right to an adequate standard of living (Article 28) and the right to health (Article 25) are important not merely because it provides a floor of social support to maintain people. It is important because it equips people with disabilities to take their own place in society and reflects a blending of the principle of nondiscrimination (immediately achievable) with obligations that are more progressive in character. What is required is that as in the normal sense government should not take a back step in implementation of these rights taking the ground of 'economic constraints.'

CHAPTER 5

CONCLUSION

The study commenced with a need to create legal awareness on visually disabled in Hubballi-Dharwad area with the understanding that violation of the rights of persons with disabilities are rampant in the society. These violations are rampant in the midst of effective legal frame work both in the International and National scenario. India is presently facing severe blindness problems and the statistics also reveals that of the total population, persons with disabilities suffering from 'seeing disability' are more compared to the other types of disabilities. Moreover, the pain and sufferings of the visually impaired are more when it comes to other kinds of disabilities as they are discriminated and excluded from the society by the same society whose dark hands remain invisible to them only... The Legislations on disability are enacted mainly with the underlying fundamental idea that society creates the barriers and oppressive structures which impede the capacities of person with disabilities. This view however, goes against the views of capability theorists like Martha Nussbaum[162] who are of the opinion that there cannot be a different set of capacities or a different threshold of capabilities for persons with disabilities. This even establishes the underlying principle of right to equality enshrined in the Constitution of India which implies that all

---

[162]Martha C. Nussbaum is currently the Ernst Freund Distinguished Service Professor of Law and Ethics appointed in the Department of Philosophy and the Law School.

citizens should have equality of fair opportunities to enable them to realise their full potential and experience well-being. To realize this, these minority groups should be made part of the society by helping them to overcome the in-built barriers created by the same society. To ensure this it is not only essential to give necessary education to the persons suffering from the disability, it is also imperative to see that such education is imparted to them in a fruitful manner. That can be achieved only if there is proper accessibility to the buildings where the educational institution is housed as well as to other facilities in the said building, namely, class rooms, library etc. Without that persons with disabilities and specifically, visually impaired would not be able to avail and utilise the educational opportunity in full measure. Thus the obligation on the part of the government is not only confined to implementing 'inclusive education' alone but should extent to habilitation and rehabilitation of persons with disabilities.

The approach of judiciary towards the protection of visually impaired has always been positive towards enabling them in realizing their rights which is reflected throughout in their decisions. In a very recent decision *Purswani Ashutosh (Minor) through Dr. Kamlsh Virumal Purswni v. Union of India& Others*[163] the Supreme Court has upheld the claim of a medical aspirant with " low vision" to be admitted in MBBS course in the category of persons with benchmark disability while holding that the provisions the RPWD Act, 2016 which consider low visibility as a benchmark disability are binding on the Medical Council of India rejecting their contention that Sec. 32 of the Act providing for reservation in higher education institutions for persons with bench mark disability only provides for reservation to higher educational

---

[163]Writ Petition (C) No (s). 669 of 2018. The question that arose in the writ petition under Art. 32 of the Constitution was whether a person with benchmark disability of low vision within the meaning of sec 2 (r) read with clause 1B of the Schedule of the Rights of Persons with Disabilities Act, 2016 can be denied the benefit of reservation for admission to the MBBS Medical Course.

institutions and not to imparting technical education. In yet another decision *Aseer Jamal v. Union of India & Ors.* the bench comprising of former CJI Dipak Misra and Justices A. M. Khanwilkar and DY Chandrachud pointed out that unreasonable classification between visually-impaired and visually- abled persons invites the frown of Art. 14 of the Constitution.[164] Further, in an elaborate judgment *Rajive Raturi v. Union of India and Others*[165] , the bench of Justice AK Sikri and Justice Ashok Bhushan has discussed the rights of visually disabled persons extensively. For effective implementation of the provisions of the RPWD Act, the bench suggested measures to be undertaken by the State authorities for removing the obstacles that prevent the disabled from accessing the public places:

(i) Making the gates to public places accessible by incorporating necessary accessible standards.[166]

(ii) Stairs to be marked with a broad yellow line to allow the visually impaired to understand the difference

(iii) Clear information about the details of the flight/train etc., should be made via public announcement systems in places like airports, railway stations etc.,

(iv) Allotting 3-5 reserved parking spaces with the international symbol for disability ie, wheelchair for persons with disabilities.

(v) Clear signposts with braille equivalents, elevators with clear signs and auditory feedback, wheelchairs and mobility scooters to be made available at every public places.

---

[164]W.P (C) No. 137 0f 2018. Here the court was analyzing Sec. 6 of the RTI Act holding that visually impaired persons should have the functional facility to receive all information as permissible under the Act.

[165]Writ Petition (Civil) No. 243 of 2005

[166]They must be made wide enough to allow wheel chairs to pass easily.

(vi) Employees working at public places should be informed of the best practices and to be provided necessary training to enable them to understand the challenges that persons with disabilities face.

In addition, the court also issued directives directing them to set deadlines to meet them.

In *Rashmi Thakur v High Court of M.P & Others* High court of Madhya Pradesh in 2017[167] asked the High Court authorities to give reservation to a visually –challenged candidate and directed it to conduct a special written examination by providing the facility of a scribe and also extra time. Chief Justice Hemant Gupta and Justice Vijay Kumar Shukla observed that the RPWD Act, 2016 has made a departure from the provisions of the earlier Act as the reservation for the physically disabled candidates is not dependent on any condition.

> The reservation can be denied only if any Government establishment is exempted from the provisions of the Act by the Chief Commissioner or the State Commissioner. In the absence of any decision to exempt the High Court from the provisions of the reservation, the High Court was bound to reserve post for the visually disabled candidates

Kerala High Court in *Prasanna Kumari E.S v The Registrar, Kannur University*[168] held that the action of the Kannur University in not considering the suitability of the petitioner for the post of lecturer in law under the quota earmarked for

---

[167]In *Rashmi Thakur v H.C of M.P and others* [Writ Petition No. 19833/2017] court followed the earlier decisions *National Federation of Blind v. U.P.S.C and Others* [AIR 1993 SC 1916]; *Indian Bank's Association, Bombay and Others v Devkala Consultancy Service* [(2004)11 SCC 1]; *Govt. of India and Another v. Ravi Prakash Gupta and Another*[(2010)7 SCC 626]; *Union of India and Another v National Federation of the Blind and others* [(2013) 10SCC 772]

[168]WP(C) No. 33953 of 2011(T)

the physically challenged candidates is clearly illegal and ruled in favour of 40 year visually impaired lady advocate who was denied the post of a lecturer by the University on the ground that she has crossed the cut-off date mentioned in the notification.

In this regard it is right to reiterate the words of Justice A.K. Sikri[169] wherein, he held:

> …..[The] gap between the laws and reality still remains. Even though human rights activists have made their best efforts to create awareness that people with disabilities have also right to enjoy their right and spend the same not only with the sense of fulfilment but also to make them contribute in the growth of the society, yet mind set of large section of the people who claimed themselves to be 'able' persons still needs to be changed towards differently abled persons

The very first chapter of the study is an introduction to the subject and its importance analysing the exact statistics and causes of blindness in India along with other factors that contribute to the growth of this minority group. The chapter has concentrated on the major and related issues faced by them in areas like (i) education (ii) skill development and employment (iii) social security, health, rehabilitation and recreation (iv) environmental barriers (v) accessibility which are glimpse of many and varied problems faced by them. The aspect highlighted throughout is that persons with disabilities do not enjoy the same opportunities in society that everybody already enjoys. These problems and discrimination is found to exist in the midst of legal frame work in the national and international scenario.

---

[169]In *Jeeja Ghosh & Another v Union of India & Ors* [W.P (C) No. 98 of 2012 Jeeja Ghosh, an eminent disability rights activist was deboarded from the Spice jet flight for having cerebral palsy.

In the second chapter an attempt has been made to analyse the struggle the persons with disabilities had to face tracing the role played by the three organs of the government namely the legislature, executive and the judiciary. All major and current legislations along with the repealed legislation and statutes on disability and also the role of administration wherein, an effort is made to analyze critically the major schemes and programmes launched and implemented by the departments/ministries of the Central/State Government for empowering the visually impaired and concluded with the approach of judiciary in recognizing the rights of the disabled. Regarding implementation of the new legislation the Office of the State Commissioner for Persons with disabilities Act – Bangalore, Karnataka, was approached to know the on-going implementation process of the newly enacted laws and its working provisions in the State. The Differently able and senior citizens welfare department was approached regarding the district level implementation of the act and in particularly the implementation of the schemes and programs in the Dharwad District for visually impaired people. Many more issues are still to be resolved in the implementation of the Act which casts an onerous duty on respective State governments.

An empirical study on the visually impaired in Hubballi-Dharwad area in the third chapter analyses the extent of legal awareness of the new legislation in all the governmental bodies including the governmental residential blind schools, employment exchange offices, certifying authorities, government aided ashrams for blind people, non-governmental organisations, charitable trusts, financial Institutions such as banks to ascertain their views to help them to become part of the society as their able bodied peers and to make suggestions to improve the quality of their lives.

Chapter Four analyses the concept of Inclusive Education tracing its evolution in the international and national scenario and aims to integrate the visually impaired with their able bodied peers with a view to harmonise the national legislation on disability in lines with the UN Disability Convention (UNCRPD) and also to analyse its adaptability in Hubballi- Dharward with the opinions gathered, from all governmental and non-governmental organizations, educational institutions, societies and Universities in the Dharwad district.

The conclusion that can be drawn from the study of the institutions scattered in Hubballi -Dharwad area has made some shocking revelations as to the problems in these institutions and the human rights violations against the visually disabled. The specific issues are listed as follows:

- **Absence of exact figures of visually disabled**

The disabled constitute the largest minority in the world and the 2011 census shows that there are 2.68 crore persons with disabilities in India who constitute 2.21% of the total population. In the State of Karnataka among the total population of 67.6 million 13,24,205 persons with disabilities are there in which, there are 2,64,170 visually impaired persons. When it comes to Hubballi-Dharwad the total population is 9, 43,788 but unfortunately the exact population of visually impaired in Hubballi-Dharwad is not available as there is absence of specific guidelines by the certifying authorities in the issue of disability certificates. The certifying authorities are designated to certify from other districts as well. Therefore, there is no certainty as to the exact figures of visually impaired.

- **Disparity in the issue of disability certificates**

The comprehensive legislation on disability the Rights of Persons with Disabilities Act, 2016 has defined visual impairment under two categories namely, blindness and low vision. India has identified major causes of blindness as cataract, malnutrition, infections, glaucoma etc., which are largely preventable or curable. However, there is gross inadequacy of qualified ophthalmologists and availability of services in rural areas. The disability certificate is the basic document that a person with any disability of 40 per cent or above requires in order to avail any facilities, benefits and concessions from the government. Karnataka Institute of Medical Sciences (KIMS) and Dharwad District hospitals have been designated as the certifying authorities in Hubballi-Dharwad area. However, disability certificate issued by the authorities will be valid only in the respective States and the requirement now is the universal validity of the disability certificates.

- **Lack of infrastructure and other adequate basic facilities to visually disabled**

The blind children in the residential schools are devoid of even proper infrastructure facilities including proper food, hygine, ramps, orientation and mobility teachers, braille teachers etc., Most of the educational institutions are not having sufficient staffs and the vacancies remain unfilled for years together. The appointments made are also not in accordance with the eligibility criteria and recruitment rules of the government. There is lack of barrier free environment with respect to accessibility and mobility of blind children. Many of these institutions revealed the lack of interest of parents and guardians in providing education for their visually disabled children but at the same time expressed their desire to get better opportunities in their struggle for recognition of their rights.

- **Increased drop-outs in educational institutions**

The right of every one to education is indisputable. It is a social right intimately connected to many other human rights. Failure to access education and training prevents the achievement of economic and social independence and increases vulnerability to poverty leading to what can become a self-perpetuating, intergenerational cycle. However, the drop-out rates of disabled children are very high. Of the persons with disabilities who are educated only 59 per cent complete class X compared to 67 per cent of the general population. In Karnataka among 2.84 lakh visually impaired persons only 10,000 are getting education and the education facilitates and other assistance provided by the State is limited up to X standard

- **Inability to implement inclusive education in educational system**

The concept of inclusive education still needs further clarification and even the question as to whether it actually helps the inclusion of children with disabilities in the mainstream is again doubtful. Most of the schools are providing education for the children with disabilities in special schools. Although the Convention speaks about inclusive education there is disparity among different ministries of the government itself. While the Ministry of Human Resource Development propagates inclusive education model where special children study in regular classrooms the Ministry of social justice and empowerment express confidence for special schools for children with special needs. The idea of integrating these children with special needs with non disabled is far from imagination in small cities like Hubballi-Dharwad.

- **Lack of individual support for visually impaired children in inclusive education system**

Despite the CRPD's high level of ratification, evidence indicates that disabled children do not get the individual support they need and remain largely unaccepted in regular schools. The situation remains the same even in the case of small cities like Hubbalii- Dharwad. Although the teachers and parents have understood the pros and cons of this concept its implementation requires an effective planning taking into consideration even the minute aspects like adequate infrastructure, staff etc. In the midst of these developments there is much opposition on the implementation of the right to inclusive education. No doubt the Act, if implemented taking adequate measure to overcome the difficulties will be accepted by the disabled community and will be a positive step towards recognizing their rights without any discrimination among those without disability.

- **Lack of awareness of latest technologies to be made accessible to visually challenged in India**

Technology has made possible to convert the print into braille, audio CDS etc., but there is a lack of awareness among all the stake holders as far as the material to be made accessible to visually challenged in India is concerned. Very few colleges and universities in India are equipped with latest technologies in the disability centre or in the academic libraries for the service of visually challenged. Various special schools were established for the visually challenged and braille text books were made available to these institutions free of cost by the government but the blind receives education free till they reach 10th standard. For obtaining higher education in India, visually impaired persons face the problem of availability of accessible reference books related to their curriculum. The libraries of higher education are still not disabled friendly. These minority groups in India feel neglected and isolated once they reach to higher education. These problems exist in the midst of International Conventions like Convention on Disability, Marrakesh treaty and other national legislations like Copyrights law, Rights of Persons with Disabilities Act, 2016 etc.,. Stressing on the role of civil society for the visually impaired National Federation of Blind (NFB), National Association for the Blind (NAB), Indian based NGOs having Blind Braille cum talking library and assistive devices of aids and appliances enable them to strive for enforcement, protection and promotion of all basic human rights including the right to education. NFB library has around 1,200 collections of books and provides braille converted language text books to maximum Universities in the State. An empirical study conducted on NGOs in the State of Karnataka has revealed that they have approached many administrative officers and ministers regarding their willingness to provide free braille text books to the visually impaired in the State for their higher studies which was promised to be considered but is still pending. Despite the lack of co-operation among the government most of the institutions and NGO's are ready to provide much support and assistance to the governmental departments in their own fields of expertise but are still not yet approached and consulted in this regard which results in the failure of the implementation of the Marrakesh treaty in its true sense. There is need for requirement of co-operation among different ministries of government, library services etc., so as to reach the benefits of access to copyrighted materials to millions of visually impaired

- **Insecurity and anxiety among the parents and children**

Above all there is increased insecurity and anxiety among the parents and children themselves in the wake of growing crimes against children because of the two conflicting views as to educate their children and the lack of awareness to procure the same in a barrier free and healthy environment. Parents themselves feel more secure in the existing situation to have their visually impaired children with them in their own home rather than getting them educated in a residential school reasonably far or near from their place of residence. The insecurity expressed by the parents of female child becomes more relevant in the light of the increasing sexual offences against the girl child in the society.

In the midst of these problems it is suggested that:

- Effective implementation of the Act is the urgent requirement of the time. However, the framing of schemes and programmes for the disabled is already delayed in the State which further requires a strong monitoring system in regulating the decision making, implementation, reporting, inspection and auditing body, in order to get the work done systematically and on time by the State Government. The need of the hour for the State Government is to decentralize all its implementations of schemes and programmes towards the District concerned authorities and proceed only with the training, inspection of its projects and assess for any further training required for its successful implementation.

- In the Centre Department of Empowerment of Persons with Disabilities was carved out of MSJE as department of disability affairs to ensure greater focus on policy matters to effectively address disability issues and to act as nodal department for greater co-ordination among stakeholders, State governments and related ministries. However, in Karnataka State the Dharwad District Disabled and Senior Citizens Welfare Department is responsible for the administration of both persons with disabilities and the senior citizens. There has to be a separate department in similar lines with the Centre for the effective implementation of the rights of disabled.

- To enable an inclusive system of education, the Government of India needs to consolidate the responsibility for education under the Ministry of Human Resource and Development and the Ministry of Social Justice and Empowerment.

- The existing norm for teacher-pupil ratio is to be increased and should not be more than 1: 10

- For effective implementation children should be put in special schools up to Vth Standard and then only to integrate in normal schools which will enable them to understand the special needs and then to adjust themselves with their non disabled peer groups.

- The disabled children, parents and the teachers of the governmental and non-governmental institutions though not legally aware of the legislations have expressed their awareness as to the facilities available under the legislations and State Government schemes and programmes. There is still the requirement to make these sections aware of their rights which is still casting an obligation on the State and the law enforcement machineries

- It is always to be understood that making adequate provisions to facilitate proper education to persons with visual impairment is to ensure that even a child with disability, after proper education, will be able to lead an independent, economically self sufficient, productive and fully participatory life.

- In India it is found that prevalence of preventable blindness are more which to an extent can be reduced by creating awareness by a team of doctors on possible available preventable measures and services more specifically in rural areas.

- Although the institutions are aware of the need for implementation of the new legislation they are equally aware of the State budgetary constraints and the difficulties of practical implications in this regard. What is required is that the phrase "to the maximum of its available resources" is not to be used as an escape route by the government for not ensuring economic social and cultural rights....

THE RIGHTS OF PERSONS WITH DISABILITIES ACT, 2016

(NO. 49 OF 2016)

[27th December, 2016]

An Act to give effect to the United Nations Convention on the Rights of Persons with Disabilities and for matters connected therewith or incidental thereto.

WHEREAS the United Nations General Assembly adopted its Convention on the Rights of Persons with Disabilities on the 13th day of December, 2006;

AND WHEREAS the aforesaid Convention lays down the following principles for empowerment of persons with disabilities, —

(a) respect for inherent dignity, individual autonomy including the freedom to make one's own choices, and independence of persons;

(b) non-discrimination;

(c) full and effective participation and inclusion in society;

(d) respect for difference and acceptance of persons with disabilities as part of human diversity and humanity;

(e) equality of opportunity;

(f) accessibility;

(g) equality between men and women;

(h) respect for the evolving capacities of children with disabilities and respect for the right of children with disabilities to preserve their identities;

AND WHEREAS India is a signatory to the said Convention;

AND WHEREAS India ratified the said Convention on the 1st day of October, 2007;

AND WHEREAS it is considered necessary to implement the Convention aforesaid.

BE it enacted by Parliament in the Sixty-seventh Year of the Republic of India as follows: —

CHAPTER I

PRELIMINARY

1. (1) This Act may be called the Rights of Persons with Disabilities Act, 2016.

(2) It shall come into force on such date as the Central Government may, by notification in the Official Gazette, appoint.

2. In this Act, unless the context otherwise requires, —

(a) "appellate authority" means an authority notified under sub-section (3) of section 14 or sub-section (1) of section 53 or designated under sub-section (1) of section 59, as the case may be;

(b) "appropriate Government" means, —

(i) in relation to the Central Government or any establishment wholly or substantially financed by that Government, or a Cantonment Board constituted under the Cantonments Act, 2006, the Central Government;

(ii) in relation to a State Government or any establishment, wholly or substantially financed by that Government, or any local authority, other than a Cantonment Board, the State Government.

(c) "barrier" means any factor including communicational, cultural, economic, environmental, institutional, political, social, attitudinal or structural factors which hampers the full and effective participation of persons with disabilities in society;

(d) "care-giver" means any person including parents and other family Members who with or without payment provides care, support or assistance to a person with disability;

(e) "certifying authority" means an authority designated under sub-section (1) of section 57;

(f) "communication" includes means and formats of communication, languages, display of text, Braille, tactile communication, signs, large print, accessible multimedia, written, audio, video, visual displays, sign language, plain-language, human-reader, augmentative and alternative modes and accessible information and communication technology;

(g) "competent authority" means an authority appointed under section 49;

(h) "discrimination" in relation to disability, means any distinction, exclusion, restriction on the basis of disability which is the purpose or effect of impairing or nullifying the recognition, enjoyment or exercise on an equal basis with others of all human rights and fundamental freedoms in the political, economic, social, cultural, civil or any other field and includes all forms of discrimination and denial of reasonable accommodation;

(i) "establishment" includes a Government establishment and private establishment;

(j) "Fund" means the National Fund constituted under section 86;

(k) "Government establishment" means a corporation established by or under a Central Act or State Act or an authority or a body owned or controlled or aided by the Government or a local authority or a Government company as defined in section 2 of the Companies Act, 2013 and includes a Department of the Government;

(l) "high support" means an intensive support, physical, psychological and otherwise, which may be required by a person with benchmark disability for daily activities, to take independent and informed decision to access facilities and participating in all areas of life including education, employment, family and community life and treatment and therapy;

(m) "inclusive education" means a system of education wherein students with and without disability learn together and the system of teaching and learning is suitably adapted to meet the learning needs of different types of students with disabilities;

(n) "information and communication technology" includes all services and innovations relating to information and communication, including telecom services, web based services, electronic and print services, digital and virtual services;

(o) "institution" means an institution for the reception, care, protection, education, training, rehabilitation and any other activities for persons with disabilities;

(p) "local authority" means a Municipality or a Panchayat, as defined in clause (e) and clause (f) of article 243P of the Constitution; a Cantonment Board constituted under the Cantonments Act, 2006; and any other authority established under an Act of Parliament or a State Legislature to administer the civic affairs;

(q) "notification" means a notification published in the Official Gazette and the expression "notify" or "notified" shall be construed accordingly;

(r) "person with benchmark disability" means a person with not less than forty per cent of a specified disability where specified disability has not been defined in measurable terms and includes a person with disability where specified disability has been defined in measurable terms, as certified by the certifying authority;

(s) "person with disability" means a person with long term physical, mental, intellectual or sensory impairment which, in interaction with barriers, hinders his full and effective participation in society equally with others;

(t) "person with disability having high support needs" means a person with benchmark disability certified under clause (a) of sub-section (2) of section 58 who needs high support;

(u) "prescribed" means prescribed by rules made under this Act;

(v) "private establishment" means a company, firm, cooperative or other society, associations, trust, agency, institution, organisation, union, factory or such other establishment as the appropriate Government may, by notification, specify;

(w) "public building" means a Government or private building, used or accessed by the public at large, including a building used for educational or vocational purposes, workplace, commercial activities, public utilities, religious, cultural, leisure or recreational activities, medical or health services, law enforcement agencies, reformatories or judicial foras, railway stations or platforms, roadways bus stands or terminus, airports or waterways;

(x) "public facilities and services" includes all forms

of delivery of services to the public at large, including housing, educational and vocational trainings, employment and career advancement, shopping or marketing, religious, cultural, leisure or recreational, medical, health and rehabilitation, banking, finance and insurance, communication, postal and information, access to justice, public utilities, transportation;

(y) "reasonable accommodation" means necessary and appropriate modification and adjustments, without imposing a disproportionate or undue burden in a particular case, to ensure to persons with disabilities the enjoyment or exercise of rights equally with others;

(z) "registered organisation" means an association of persons with disabilities or a disabled person organisation, association of parents of persons with disabilities, association of persons with disabilities and family members, or a voluntary or non-governmental or charitable organisation or trust, society, or non-profit company working for the welfare of the persons with disabilities, duly registered under an Act of Parliament or a State Legislature;

(za) "rehabilitation" refers to a process aimed at enabling persons with disabilities to attain and maintain optimal, physical, sensory, intellectual, psychological environmental or social function levels;

(zb) "Special Employment Exchange" means any office or place established and maintained by the Government for the collection and furnishing of information, either by keeping of registers or otherwise, regarding—

(i) persons who seek to engage employees from amongst the persons with disabilities;

(ii) persons with benchmark disability who seek employment;

(iii) vacancies to which persons with benchmark disabilities seeking employment may be appointed;

(zc) "specified disability" means the disabilities as specified in the Schedule;

(zd) "transportation systems" includes road transport, rail transport, air transport, water transport, para transit systems for the last mile connectivity, road and street infrastructure, etc.;

(ze) "universal design" means the design of products, environments, programmes and services to be usable by all people to the greatest extent possible, without the need for adaptation or specialised design and shall apply to assistive devices including advanced technologies for particular group of persons with disabilities.

CHAPTER II

RIGHTS AND ENTITLEMENTS

3. (1) The appropriate Government shall ensure that the persons with disabilities enjoy the right to equality, life with dignity and respect for his or her integrity equally with others.

(2) The appropriate Government shall take steps to utilise the capacity of persons with disabilities by providing appropriate environment.

(3) No person with disability shall be discriminated on the ground of disability, unless it is shown that the impugned act or omission is a proportionate means of achieving a legitimate aim.

(4) No person shall be deprived of his or her personal liberty only on the ground of disability.

(5) The appropriate Government shall take necessary

steps to ensure reasonable accommodation for persons with disabilities.

4. (1) The appropriate Government and the local authorities shall take measures to ensure that the women and children with disabilities enjoy their rights equally with others.

(2) The appropriate Government and local authorities shall ensure that all children with disabilities shall have right on an equal basis to freely express their views on all matters affecting them and provide them appropriate support keeping in view their age and disability.".

5. (1) The persons with disabilities shall have the right to live in the community.

(2) The appropriate Government shall endeavour that the persons with disabilities are,—

(a) not obliged to live in any particular living arrangement; and

(b) given access to a range of in-house, residential and other community support services, including personal assistance necessary to support living with due regard to age and gender.

6. (1) The appropriate Government shall take measures to protect persons with disabilities from being subjected to torture, cruel, inhuman or degrading treatment.

(2) No person with disability shall be a subject of any research without,—

(i) his or her free and informed consent obtained through accessible modes, means and formats of communication; and

(ii) prior permission of a Committee for Research on Disability constituted in the prescribed manner for the purpose by the appropriate Government in which not less than half of the Members shall themselves be either persons with disabilities or Members of the registered organisation as defined under clause (z) of section 2.

7. (1) The appropriate Government shall take measures to protect persons with disabilities from all forms of abuse, violence and exploitation and to prevent the same, shall —

(a) take cognizance of incidents of abuse, violence and exploitation and provide legal remedies available against such incidents;

(b) take steps for avoiding such incidents and prescribe the procedure for its reporting;

(c) take steps to rescue, protect and rehabilitate victims of such incidents; and

(d) create awareness and make available information among the public.

(2) Any person or registered organisation who or which has reason to believe that an act of abuse, violence or exploitation has been, or is being, or is likely to be committed against any person with disability, may give information about it to the Executive Magistrate within the local limits of whose jurisdiction such incidents occur.

(3) The Executive Magistrate on receipt of such information, shall take immediate steps to stop or prevent its occurrence, as the case may be, or pass such order as he deems fit for the protection of such person with disability including an order —

(a) to rescue the victim of such act, authorising the police or any organization working for persons with disabilities to provide for the safe custody or rehabilitation of such person, or both, as the case may be;

(b) for providing protective custody to the person with

disability, if such person so desires;

(c) to provide maintenance to such person with disability.

(4) Any police officer who receives a complaint or otherwise comes to know of abuse, violence or exploitation towards any person with disability shall inform the aggrieved person of —

(a) his or her right to apply for protection under sub-section (2) and the particulars of the Executive Magistrate having jurisdiction to provide assistance;

(b) the particulars of the nearest organisation or institution working for the rehabilitation of persons with disabilities;

(c) the right to free legal aid; and

(d) the right to file a complaint under the provisions of this Act or any other law dealing with such offence:

Provided that nothing in this section shall be construed in any manner as to relieve the police officer from his duty to proceed in accordance with law upon receipt of information as to the commission of a cognizable offence.

(5) If the Executive Magistrate finds that the alleged act or behaviour constitutes an offence under the Indian Penal Code, or under any other law for the time being in force, he may forward the complaint to that effect to the Judicial or Metropolitan Magistrate, as the case may be, having jurisdiction in the matter.

8. (1) The persons with disabilities shall have equal protection and safety in situations of risk, armed conflict, humanitarian emergencies and natural disasters.

(2) The National Disaster Management Authority and the State Disaster Management Authority shall take appropriate measures to ensure inclusion of persons with

disabilities in its disaster management activities as defined under clause (e) of section 2 of the Disaster Management Act, 2005 for the safety and protection of persons with disabilities.

(3) The District Disaster Management Authority constituted under section 25 of the Disaster Management Act, 2005 shall maintain record of details of persons with disabilities in the district and take suitable measures to inform such persons of any situations of risk so as to enhance disaster preparedness.

(4) The authorities engaged in reconstruction activities subsequent to any situation of risk, armed conflict or natural disasters shall undertake such activities, in consultation with the concerned State Commissioner, in accordance with the accessibility requirements of persons with disabilities.

9. (1)   No child with disability shall be separated from his or her parents on the ground of disability except on an order of competent court, if required, in the best interest of the child.

(2)   Where the parents are unable to take care of a child with disability, the competent court shall place such child with his or her near relations, and failing that within the community in a family setting or in exceptional cases in shelter home run by the appropriate Government or non-governmental organisation, as may be required.

10. (1) The appropriate Government shall ensure that persons with disabilities have access to appropriate information regarding reproductive and family planning.

(2) No person with disability shall be subject to any medical procedure which leads to infertility without his or her free and informed consent.

11.   The Election Commission of India and the State

Election Commissions shall ensure that all polling stations are accessible to persons with disabilities and all materials related to the electoral process are easily understandable by and accessible to them.

12. (1) The appropriate Government shall ensure that persons with disabilities are able to exercise the right to access any court, tribunal, authority, commission or any other body having judicial or quasi-judicial or investigative powers without discrimination on the basis of disability.

(2) The appropriate Government shall take steps to put in place suitable support measures for persons with disabilities specially those living outside family and those disabled requiring high support for exercising legal rights.

(3) The National Legal Services Authority and the State Legal Services Authorities constituted under the Legal Services Authorities Act, 1987 shall make provisions including reasonable accommodation to ensure that persons with disabilities have access to any scheme, programme, facility or service offered by them equally with others.

(4) The appropriate Government shall take steps to —

(a) ensure that all their public documents are in accessible formats;

(b) ensure that the filing departments, registry or any other office of records are supplied with necessary equipment to enable filing, storing and referring to the documents and evidence in accessible formats; and

(c) make available all necessary facilities and equipment to facilitate recording of testimonies, arguments or opinion given by persons with disabilities in their preferred language and means of communication.

13. (1) The appropriate Government shall ensure that the persons with disabilities have right, equally with others, to own or inherit property, movable or immovable, control their financial affairs and have access to bank loans, mortgages and other forms of financial credit.

(2) The appropriate Government shall ensure that the persons with disabilities enjoy legal capacity on an equal basis with others in all aspects of life and have the right to equal recognition everywhere as any other person before the law.

(3) When a conflict of interest arises between a person providing support and a person with disability in a particular financial, property or other economic transaction, then such supporting person shall abstain from providing support to the person with disability in that transaction:

Provided that there shall not be a presumption of conflict of interest just on the basis that the supporting person is related to the person with disability by blood, affinity or adoption.

(4) A person with disability may alter, modify or dismantle any support arrangement and seek the support of another:

Provided that such alteration, modification or dismantling shall be prospective in nature and shall not nullify any third party transaction entered into by the person with disability with the aforesaid support arrangement.

(5) Any person providing support to the person with disability shall not exercise undue influence and shall respect his or her autonomy, dignity and privacy.

14. (1) Notwithstanding anything contained in any other law for the time being in force, on and from the date of commencement of this Act, where a district court or any designated authority, as notified by the State Government, finds that a person with disability, who had been provided

adequate and appropriate support but is unable to take legally binding decisions, may be provided further support of a limited guardian to take legally binding decisions on his behalf in consultation with such person, in such manner, as may be prescribed by the State Government:

Provided that the District Court or the designated authority, as the case may be, may grant total support to the person with disability requiring such support or where the limited guardianship is to be granted repeatedly, in which case, the decision regarding the support to be provided shall be reviewed by the Court or the designated authority, as the case may be, to determine the nature and manner of support to be provided.

Explanation. — For the purposes of this sub-section, "limited guardianship" means a system of joint decision which operates on mutual understanding and trust between the guardian and the person with disability, which shall be limited to a specific period and for specific decision and situation and shall operate in accordance to the will of the person with disability.

(2) On and from the date of commencement of this Act, every guardian appointed under any provision of any other law for the time being in force, for a person with disability shall be deemed to function as a limited guardian.

(3) Any person with disability aggrieved by the decision of the designated authority appointing a legal guardian may prefer an appeal to such appellate authority, as may be notified by the State Government for the purpose.

15. (1) The appropriate Government shall designate one or more authorities to mobilize the community and create social awareness to support persons with disabilities in exercise of their legal capacity.

(2) The authority designated under sub-section (1) shall take measures for setting up suitable support arrangements to exercise legal capacity by persons with disabilities living in institutions and those with high support needs and any other measures as may be required.

CHAPTER III

EDUCATION

16. The appropriate Government and the local authorities shall endeavour that all educational institutions funded or recognised by them provide inclusive education to the children with disabilities and towards that end shall —

(i) admit them without discrimination and provide education and opportunities for sports and recreation activities equally with others;

(ii) make building, campus and various facilities accessible;

(iii) provide reasonable accommodation according to the individual's requirements;

(iv) provide necessary support individualised or otherwise in environments that maximise academic and social development consistent with the goal of full inclusion;

(v) ensure that the education to persons who are blind or deaf or both is imparted in the most appropriate languages and modes and means of communication;

(vi) detect specific learning disabilities in children at the earliest and take suitable pedagogical and other measures to overcome them;

(vii) monitor participation, progress in terms of attainment levels and completion of education in respect of every student with disability;

(viii) provide transportation facilities to the children with disabilities and also the attendant of the children with disabilities having high support needs.

17. The appropriate Government and the local authorities shall take the following measures for the purpose of section 16, namely:—

(a) to conduct survey of school going children in every five years for identifying children with disabilities, ascertaining their special needs and the extent to which these are being met:

Provided that the first survey shall be conducted within a period of two years from the date of commencement of this Act;

(b) to establish adequate number of teacher training institutions;

(c) to train and employ teachers, including teachers with disability who are qualified in sign language and Braille and also teachers who are trained in teaching children with intellectual disability;

(d) to train professionals and staff to support inclusive education at all levels of school education;

(e) to establish adequate number of resource centres to support educational institutions at all levels of school education;

(f) to promote the use of appropriate augmentative and alternative modes including means and formats of communication, Braille and sign language to supplement the use of one's own speech to fulfill the daily communication needs of persons with speech, communication or language disabilities and enables them to participate and contribute to their community and society;

(g) to provide books, other learning materials and appropriate assistive devices to students with benchmark disabilities free of cost up to the age of eighteen years;

(h) to provide scholarships in appropriate cases to students with benchmark disability;

(i) to make suitable modifications in the curriculum and examination system to meet the needs of students with disabilities such as extra time for completion of examination paper, facility of scribe or amanuensis, exemption from second and third language courses;

(j) to promote research to improve learning; and

(k) any other measures, as may be required.

18. The appropriate Government and the local authorities shall take measures to promote, protect and ensure participation of persons with disabilities in adult education and continuing education programmes equally with others.

CHAPTER IV

SKILL DEVELOPMENT AND EMPLOYMENT

19. (1) The appropriate Government shall formulate schemes and programmes including provision of loans at concessional rates to facilitate and support employment of persons with disabilities especially for their vocational training and self-employment.

(2) The schemes and programmes referred to in sub-section (1) shall provide for —

(a) inclusion of person with disability in all mainstream formal and non-formal vocational and skill training schemes and programmes;

(b) to ensure that a person with disability has adequate support and facilities to avail specific training;

(c) exclusive skill training programmes for persons with disabilities with active links with the market, for those with developmental, intellectual, multiple disabilities and autism;

(d) loans at concessional rates including that of microcredit;

(e) marketing the products made by persons with disabilities; and

(f) maintenance of disaggregated data on the progress made in the skill training and self-employment, including persons with disabilities.

20. (1) No Government establishment shall discriminate

against any person with disability in any matter
relating to employment:

Provided that the appropriate Government may, having regard to the type of work carried on in any establishment, by notification and subject to such conditions, if any, exempt any establishment from the provisions of this section.

(2) Every Government establishment shall provide reasonable accommodation and appropriate barrier free and conducive environment to employees with disability.

(3) No promotion shall be denied to a person merely on the ground of disability.

(4) No Government establishment shall dispense with or reduce in rank, an employee who acquires a disability during his or her service:

Provided that, if an employee after acquiring disability is not suitable for the post he was holding, shall be shifted to some other post with the same pay scale and service benefits:

Provided further that if it is not possible to adjust the employee against any post, he may be kept on a supernumerary post until a suitable post is available or he attains the age of superannuation, whichever is earlier.

(5) The appropriate Government may frame policies for posting and transfer of employees with disabilities.

21. (1) Every establishment shall notify equal opportunity policy detailing measures proposed to be taken by it in pursuance of the provisions of this Chapter in the manner as may be prescribed by the Central Government.

(2) Every establishment shall register a copy of the said policy with the Chief Commissioner or the State Commissioner, as the case may be.

22. (1) Every establishment shall maintain records of the persons with disabilities in relation to the matter of employment, facilities provided and other necessary information in compliance with the provisions of this Chapter in such form and manner as may be prescribed by the Central Government.

(2) Every employment exchange shall maintain records of persons with disabilities seeking employment.

(3) The records maintained under sub-section (1) shall be open to inspection at all reasonable hours by such persons as may be authorised in their behalf by the appropriate Government.

23. (1) Every Government establishment shall appoint a Grievance Redressal Officer for the purpose of section 19 and shall inform the Chief Commissioner or the State Commissioner, as the case may be, about the appointment of such officer.

(2) Any person aggrieved with the non-compliance of the provisions of section 20, may file a complaint with

the Grievance Redressal Officer, who shall investigate it and shall take up the matter with the establishment for corrective action.

(3) The Grievance Redressal Officer shall maintain a register of complaints in the manner as may be prescribed by the Central Government, and every complaint shall be inquired within two weeks of its registration.

(4) If the aggrieved person is not satisfied with the action taken on his or her complaint, he or she may approach the District-Level Committee on disability.

CHAPTER V

SOCIAL SECURITY, HEALTH, REHABILITATION AND RECREATION

24. (1) The appropriate Government shall within the limit of its economic capacity and development formulate necessary schemes and programmes to safeguard and promote the right of persons with disabilities for adequate standard of living to enable them to live independently or in the community:

Provided that the quantum of assistance to the persons with disabilities under such schemes and programmes shall be at least twenty-five per cent. higher than the similar schemes applicable to others.

(2) The appropriate Government while devising these schemes and programmes shall give due consideration to the diversity of disability, gender, age, and socio-economic status.

(3) The schemes under sub-section (1) shall provide for,—

(a) community centres with good living conditions in terms of safety, sanitation, health care and counselling;

(b) facilities for persons including children with disabilities who have no family or have been abandoned, or are without shelter or livelihood;

(c) support during natural or man-made disasters and in areas of conflict;

(d) support to women with disability for livelihood and for upbringing of their children;

(e) access to safe drinking water and appropriate and accessible sanitation facilities especially in urban slums and rural areas;

(f) provisions of aids and appliances, medicine and diagnostic services and corrective surgery free of cost to persons with disabilities with such income ceiling as may be notified;

(g) disability pension to persons with disabilities subject to such income ceiling as may be notified;

(h) unemployment allowance to persons with disabilities registered with Special Employment Exchange for more than two years and who could not be placed in any gainful occupation;

(i) care-giver allowance to persons with disabilities with high support needs;

(j) comprehensive insurance scheme for persons with disability, not covered under the Employees State Insurance Schemes, or any other statutory or Government sponsored insurance schemes;

(k) any other matter which the appropriate Government may think fit.

25. (1) The appropriate Government and the local authorities shall take necessary measures for the persons with disabilities to provide, —

(a) free healthcare in the vicinity specially in rural area

subject to such family income as may be notified;

(b) barrier-free access in all parts of Government and private hospitals and other healthcare institutions and centres;

(c) priority in attendance and treatment.

(2) The appropriate Government and the local authorities shall take measures and make schemes or programmes to promote healthcare and prevent the occurrence of disabilities and for the said purpose shall —

(a) undertake or cause to be undertaken surveys, investigations and research concerning the cause of occurrence of disabilities;

(b) promote various methods for preventing disabilities;

(c) screen all the children at least once in a year for the purpose of identifying

"at-risk" cases;

(d) provide facilities for training to the staff at the primary health centres;

(e) sponsor or cause to be sponsored awareness campaigns and disseminate or cause to be disseminated information for general hygiene, health and sanitation;

(f) take measures for pre-natal, perinatal and post-natal care of mother and child;

(g) educate the public through the pre-schools, schools, primary health centres, village level workers and anganwadi workers;

(h) create awareness amongst the masses through television, radio and other mass media on the causes of disabilities and the preventive measures to be adopted;

(i) healthcare during the time of natural disasters and other situations of risk;

(j) essential medical facilities for life saving emergency treatment and procedures; and

(k) sexual and reproductive healthcare especially for women with disability.

26. The appropriate Government shall, by notification, make insurance schemes for their employees with disabilities.

27. (1) The appropriate Government and the local authorities shall within their economic capacity and development, undertake or cause to be undertaken services and programmes of rehabilitation, particularly in the areas of health, education and employment for all persons with disabilities.

(2) For the purposes of sub-section (1), the appropriate Government and the local authorities may grant financial assistance to non-Governmental Organisations.

(3) The appropriate Government and the local authorities, while formulating rehabilitation policies shall consult the non-Governmental Organisations working for the cause of persons with disabilities.

28. The appropriate Government shall initiate or cause to be initiated research and development through individuals and institutions on issues which shall enhance habilitation and rehabilitation and on such other issues which are necessary for the empowerment of persons with disabilities.

29. The appropriate Government and the local authorities shall take measures to promote and protect the rights of all persons with disabilities to have a cultural life and to participate in recreational activities equally with others which include, —

(a) facilities, support and sponsorships to artists and

writers with disability to pursue their interests and talents;

(b) establishment of a disability history museum which chronicles and interprets the historical experiences of persons with disabilities;

(c) making art accessible to persons with disabilities;

(d) promoting recreation centres, and other associational activities;

(e) facilitating participation in scouting, dancing, art classes, outdoor camps and adventure activities;

(f) redesigning courses in cultural and arts subjects to enable participation and access for persons with disabilities;

(g) developing technology, assistive devices and equipments to facilitate access and inclusion for persons with disabilities in recreational activities; and

(h) ensuring that persons with hearing impairment can have access to television programmes with sign language interpretation or sub-titles.

30. (1) The appropriate Government shall take measures to ensure effective participation in sporting activities of the persons with disabilities.

(2) The sports authorities shall accord due recognition to the right of persons with disabilities to participate in sports and shall make due provisions for the inclusion of persons with disabilities in their schemes and programmes for the promotion and development of sporting talents.

(3) Without prejudice to the provisions contained in sub-sections (1) and (2), the appropriate Government and the sports authorities shall take measures to, —

(a) restructure courses and programmes to ensure access, inclusion and participation of persons with disabilities in all sporting activities;

(b) redesign and support infrastructure facilities of all sporting activities for persons with disabilities;

(c) develop technology to enhance potential, talent, capacity and ability in sporting activities of all persons with disabilities;

(d) provide multi-sensory essentials and features in all sporting activities to ensure effective participation of all persons with disabilities;

(e) allocate funds for development of state of art sport facilities for training of persons with disabilities;

(f) promote and organise disability specific sporting events for persons with disabilities and also facilitate awards to the winners and other participants of such sporting events.

CHAPTER VI

SPECIAL PROVISIONS FOR PERSONS WITH BENCHMARK DISABIILITES

31. (1) Notwithstanding anything contained in the Rights of Children to Free and Compulsory Education Act, 2009, every child with benchmark disability between the age of six to eighteen years shall have the right to free education in a neighbourhood school, or in a special school, of his choice.

(2) The appropriate Government and local authorities shall ensure that every child with benchmark disability has access to free education in an appropriate environment till he attains the age of eighteen years.

32. (1) All Government institutions of higher education and other higher education institutions receiving aid from the

Government shall reserve not less than five per cent. Seats for persons with benchmark disabilities.

(2) The persons with benchmark disabilities shall be given an upper age relaxation of five years for admission in institutions of higher education.

33. The appropriate Government shall —

(i) identify posts in the establishments which can be held by respective category of persons with benchmark disabilities in respect of the vacancies reserved in accordance with the provisions of section 34;

(ii) constitute an expert committee with representation of persons with benchmark disabilities for identification of such posts; and

(iii) undertake periodic review of the identified posts at an interval not exceeding three years.

34. (1) Every appropriate Government shall appoint in every Government establishment, not less than four per cent. of the total number of vacancies in the cadre strength in each group of posts meant to be filled with persons with benchmark disabilities of which, one per cent. each shall be reserved for persons with benchmark disabilities under clauses (a), (b) and (c) and one per cent. for persons with benchmark disabilities under clauses (d) and (e), namely: —

(a) blindness and low vision;

(b) deaf and hard of hearing;

(c) locomotor disability including cerebral palsy, leprosy cured, dwarfism, acid attack victims and muscular dystrophy;

(d) autism, intellectual disability, specific learning disability and mental illness;

(e) multiple disabilities from amongst persons under

clauses (a) to (d) including deaf-blindness in the posts identified for each disabilities:

Provided that the reservation in promotion shall be in accordance with such instructions as are issued by the appropriate Government from time to time:

Provided further that the appropriate Government, in consultation with the Chief Commissioner or the State Commissioner, as the case may be, may, having regard to the type of work carried out in any Government establishment, by notification and subject to such conditions, if any, as may be specified in such notifications exempt any Government establishment from the provisions of this section.

(2) Where in any recruitment year any vacancy cannot be filled up due to non availability of a suitable person with benchmark disability or for any other sufficient reasons, such vacancy shall be carried forward in the succeeding recruitment year and if in the succeeding recruitment year also suitable person with benchmark disability is not available, it may first be filled by interchange among the five categories and only when there is no person with disability available for the post in that year, the employer shall fill up the vacancy by appointment of a person, other than a person with disability:

Provided that if the nature of vacancies in an establishment is such that a given category of person cannot be employed, the vacancies may be interchanged among the five categories with the prior approval of the appropriate Government.

(3) The appropriate Government may, by notification, provide for such relaxation of upper age limit for employment of persons with benchmark disability, as it thinks fit.

35. The appropriate Government and the local authorities shall, within the limit of their economic capacity and development, provide incentives to employer in private sector to ensure that at least five per cent. of their work force is composed of persons with benchmark disability.

36. The appropriate Government may, by notification, require that from such date, the employer in every establishment shall furnish such information or return as may be prescribed by the Central Government in relation to vacancies appointed for persons with benchmark disability that have occurred or are about to occur in that establishment to such special employment exchange as may be notified by the Central Government and the establishment shall thereupon comply with such requisition.

37. The appropriate Government and the local authorities shall, by notification, make schemes in favour of persons with benchmark disabilities, to provide, —

(a) five per cent. reservation in allotment of agricultural land and housing in all relevant schemes and development programmes, with appropriate priority to women with benchmark disabilities;

(b) five per cent. reservation in all poverty alleviation and various developmental schemes with priority to women with benchmark disabilities;

(c) five per cent. reservation in allotment of land on concessional rate, where such land is to be used for the purpose of promoting housing, shelter, setting up of occupation, business, enterprise, recreation centres and production centres.

CHAPTER VII

SPECIAL PROVISIONS FOR PERSONS WITH DISABILITIES
WITH HIGH SUPPORT NEEDS

38. (1) Any person with benchmark disability, who considers himself to be in need of high support, or any person or organisation on his or her behalf, may apply to an authority, to be notified by the appropriate Government, requesting to provide high support.

(2) On receipt of an application under sub-section (1), the authority shall refer it to an Assessment Board consisting of such Members as may be prescribed by the Central Government.

(3) The Assessment Board shall assess the case referred to it under sub-section (1) in such manner as may be prescribed by the Central Government, and shall send a report to the authority certifying the need of high support and its nature.

(4) On receipt of a report under sub-section (3), the authority shall take steps to provide support in accordance with the report and subject to relevant schemes and orders of the appropriate Government in this behalf.

CHAPTER VIII

DUTIES AND RESPONSIBILITIES OF APPROPRIATE GOVERNMENTS

39. (1) The appropriate Government, in consultation with the Chief Commissioner or the StateCommissioner, as the case may be, shall conduct, encourage, support or promote awareness campaigns and sensitisation programmes to ensure that the rights of the persons with disabilities provided under this Act are protected.

(2) The programmes and campaigns specified under sub-section (1) shall also, —

(a) promote values of inclusion, tolerance, empathy and respect for diversity;

(b) advance recognition of the skills, merits and abilities of persons with disabilities and of their contributions to the workforce, labour market and professional fee;

(c) foster respect for the decisions made by persons with disabilities on all matters related to family life, relationships, bearing and raising children;

(d) provide orientation and sensitisation at the school, college, University and professional training level on the human condition of disability and the rights of persons with disabilities;

(e) provide orientation and sensitisation on disabling conditions and rights of persons with disabilities to employers, administrators and co-workers;

(f) ensure that the rights of persons with disabilities are included in the curriculum in Universities, colleges and schools.

40. The Central Government shall, in consultation with the Chief Commissioner, formulate rules for persons with disabilities laying down the standards of accessibility for the physical environment, transportation, information and communications, including appropriate technologies and systems, and other facilities and services provided to the public in urban and rural areas.

41. (1) The appropriate Government shall take suitable measures to provide, —

(a) facilities for persons with disabilities at bus stops, railway stations and airports conforming to the accessibility standards relating to parking spaces, toilets, ticketing counters and ticketing machines;

(b) access to all modes of transport that conform the design standards, including retrofitting old modes of transport, wherever technically feasible and safe for persons with disabilities, economically viable and without entailing major structural changes in design;

(c) accessible roads to address mobility necessary for persons with disabilities.

(2) The appropriate Government shall develop schemes programmes to promote the personal mobility of persons with disabilities at affordable cost to provide for, —

(a) incentives and concessions;

(b) retrofitting of vehicles; and

(c) personal mobility assistance.

42. The appropriate Government shall take measures to ensure that, —

(i) all contents available in audio, print and electronic media are in accessible format;

(ii) persons with disabilities have access to electronic media by providing audio description, sign language interpretation and close captioning;

(iii) electronic goods and equipment which are meant for every day use are available in universal design.

43. The appropriate Government shall take measures to promote development, production and distribution of universally designed consumer products and accessories for general use for persons with disabilities.

44. (1) No establishment shall be granted permission to build any structure if the building plan does not adhere to the rules formulated by the Central Government under section 40.

(2) No establishment shall be issued a certificate of completion or allowed to take occupation of a building unless it has adhered to the rules formulated by the Central Government.

45. (1) All existing public buildings shall be made accessible in accordance with the rules formulated by the Central Government within a period not exceeding five years from the date of notification of such rules:

Provided that the Central Government may grant extension of time to the States on a case to case basis for adherence to this provision depending on their state of preparedness and other related parameters.

(2) The appropriate Government and the local authorities shall formulate and publish an action plan based on prioritisation, for providing accessibility in all their buildings and spaces providing essential services such as all primary health centres, civil hospitals, schools, railway stations and bus stops.

46. The service providers whether Government or private shall provide services in accordance with the rules on accessibility formulated by the Central Government under section 40 within a period of two years from the date of notification of such rules:

Provided that the Central Government in consultation with the Chief Commissioner may grant extension of time for providing certain category of services in accordance with the said rules.

47. (1) Without prejudice to any function and power of Rehabilitation Council of India constituted under the Rehabilitation Council of India Act, 1992, the appropriate Government shall endeavour to develop human resource for the purposes of this Act and to that end shall, —

(a) mandate training on disability rights in all courses for the training of Panchayati Raj Members, legislators, administrators, police officials, judges and lawyers;

(b) induct disability as a component for all education courses for schools, colleges and University teachers, doctors, nurses, para-medical personnel, social welfare officers, rural development officers, asha workers, anganwadi workers, engineers, architects, other professionals and community workers;

(c) initiate capacity building programmes including training in independent living and community relationships for families, members of community and other stakeholders and care providers on care giving and support;

(d) ensure independence training for persons with disabilities to build community relationships on mutual contribution and respect;

(e) conduct training programmes for sports teachers with focus on sports, games, adventure activities;

(f) any other capacity development measures as may be required.

(2) All Universities shall promote teaching and research in disability studies including establishment of study centres for such studies.

(3) In order to fulfil the obligation stated in sub-section (1), the appropriate Government shall in every five years undertake a need based analysis and formulate plans for the recruitment, induction, sensitisation, orientation and training of suitable personnel to undertake the various responsibilities under this Act.

48. The appropriate Government shall undertake social audit of all general schemes and programmes involving the persons with disabilities to ensure that the scheme and programmes do not have an adverse impact upon the persons with disabilities and need the requirements and concerns of persons with disabilities.

CHAPTER IX

REGISTRATION OF INSTITUTIONS FOR PERSONS WITH

DISABILITIES AND GRANTS TO SUCH INSTITUTIONS

49. The State Government shall appoint an authority as it deems fit to be a competent authority for the purposes of this Chapter.

50. Save as otherwise provided under this Act, no person shall establish or maintain any institution for persons with disabilities except in accordance with a certificate of registration issued in this behalf by the competent authority:

Provided that an institution for care of mentally ill persons, which holds a valid licence under section 8 of the Mental Health Act, 1987 or any other Act for the time being in force, shall not be required to be registered under this Act.

51. (1) Every application for a certificate of registration shall be made to the competent authority in such form and in such manner as may be prescribed by the State Government.

(2) On receipt of an application under sub-section (1), the competent authority shall make such enquiries as it may deem fit and on being satisfied that the applicant has complied with the requirements of this Act and the rules made there under, it shall grant a certificate of registration to the applicant within a period of ninety days of receipt of application and if not satisfied, the competent authority shall, by order, refuse to grant the certificate applied for:

Provided that before making any order refusing to grant a certificate, the competent authority shall give the applicant a reasonable opportunity of being heard and every order of refusal to grant a certificate shall be communicated to the applicant in writing.

(3) No certificate of registration shall be granted under

sub-section (2) unless the institution with respect to which an application has been made is in a position to provide such facilities and meet such standards as may be prescribed by the State Government.

(4) The certificate of registration granted under sub-section (2) , –

(a) shall, unless revoked under section 52 remain in force for such period as may be prescribed by the State Government;

(b) may be renewed from time to time for a like period; and

(c) shall be in such form and shall be subject to such conditions as may beprescribed by the State Government.

(5) An application for renewal of a certificate of registration shall be made not less than sixty days before the expiry of the period of validity.

(6) A copy of the certificate of registration shall be displayed by the institution in a conspicuous place.

(7) Every application made under sub-section (1) or sub-section (5) shall be disposed of by the competent authority within such period as may be prescribed by the State Government.

52. (1) The competent authority may, if it has reason to believe that the holder of a certificate of registration granted under sub-section (2) of section 51 has, –

(a) made a statement in relation to any application for the issue or renewal of the certificate which is incorrect or false in material particulars; or

(b) committed or has caused to be committed any breach of rules or any conditions subject to which the certificate was granted, it may, after making such inquiry, as it deems fit, by order, revoke the certificate:

Provided that no such order shall be made until an opportunity is given to the holder of the certificate to show cause as to why the certificate of registration shall not be revoked.

(2) Where a certificate of registration in respect of an institution has been revoked under sub-section (1), such institution shall cease to function from the date of such revocation:

Provided that where an appeal lies under section 53 against the order of revocation, such institution shall cease to function, —

(a) where no appeal has been preferred immediately on the expiry of the period prescribed for the filing of such appeal; or

(b) where such appeal has been preferred, but the order of revocation has been upheld, from the date of the order of appeal.

(3) On the revocation of a certificate of registration in respect of an institution, the competent authority may direct that any person with disability who is an inmate of such institution on the date of such revocation, shall be —

(a) restored to the custody of his or her parent, spouse or lawful guardian, as the case may be; or

(b) transferred to any other institution specified by the competent authority.

(4) Every institution which holds a certificate of registration which is revoked under this section shall, immediately after such revocation, surrender such certificate to the competent authority.

53. (1) Any person aggrieved by the order of the competent authority refusing to grant a certificate of registration or revoking a certificate of registration may, within such period as may be prescribed by the State Government, prefer an appeal to such appellate authority, as may be notified by the State Government against such refusal or revocation.

(2) The order of the appellate authority on such appeal shall be final.

54. Nothing contained in this Chapter shall apply to an institution for persons with disabilities established or maintained by the Central Government or a State Government.

55. The appropriate Government may within the limits of their economic capacity and development, grant financial assistance to registered institutions to provide services and to implement the schemes and programmes in pursuance of the provisions of this Act.

CHAPTER X

CERTIFICATION OF SPECIFIED DISABILITIES

56. The Central Government shall notify guidelines for the purpose of assessing the extent of specified disability in a person.

57. (1) The appropriate Government shall designate persons, having requisite qualifications and experience, as certifying authorities, who shall be competent to issue the certificate of disability.

(2) The appropriate Government shall also notify the jurisdiction within which and the terms and conditions subject to which, the certifying authority shall perform its certification functions.

58. (1) Any person with specified disability, may apply, in such manner as may be prescribed by the Central

Government, to a certifying authority having jurisdiction, for issuing of a certificate of disability.

(2) On receipt of an application under sub-section (1), the certifying authority shall assess the disability of the concerned person in accordance with relevant guidelines notified under section 56, and shall, after such assessment, as the case may be, —

(a) issue a certificate of disability to such person, in such form as may be prescribed by the Central Government;

(b) inform him in writing that he has no specified disability.

(3) The certificate of disability issued under this section shall be valid across the country.

59. (1) Any person aggrieved with decision of the certifying authority, may appeal against such decision, within such time and in such manner as may be prescribed by the State Government, to such appellate authority as the State Government may designate for the purpose.

(2) On receipt of an appeal, the appellate authority shall decide the appeal in such manner as may be prescribed by the State Government.

CHAPTER XI

CENTRAL AND STATE ADVISORY BOARDS ON DISABILITY
AND DISTRICT LEVEL COMMITTEE

60. (1) The Central Government shall, by notification, constitute a body to be known as the Central Advisory Board on Disability to exercise the powers conferred on, and to perform the functions assigned to it, under this Act.

(2) The Central Advisory Board shall consist of, —

(a) the Minister in charge of Department of Disability Affairs in the Central Government, Chairperson, ex officio;

(b) the Minister of State in charge dealing with Department of Disability Affairs in the Ministry in the Central Government, Vice Chairperson, ex officio;

(c) three Members of Parliament, of whom two shall be elected by Lok Sabha and one by the Rajya Sabha, Members, ex officio;

(d) the Ministers in charge of Disability Affairs of all States and Administrators or Lieutenant Governors of the Union territories, Members, ex officio;

(e) Secretaries to the Government of India in charge of the Ministries or Departments of Disability Affairs, Social Justice and Empowerment, School Education and Literacy, and Higher Education, Women and Child Development, Expenditure, Personnel and Training, Administrative Reforms and Public Grievances, Health and Family Welfare, Rural Development, Panchayati Raj, Industrial Policy and Promotion, Urban Development, Housing and Urban Poverty Alleviation, Science and Technology, Communications and Information Technology, Legal Affairs, Public Enterprises, Youth Affairs and Sports, Road Transport and Highways and Civil Aviation, Members, ex officio;

(f) Secretary, National Institute of Transforming India (NITI) Aayog, Member, ex officio;

(g) Chairperson, Rehabilitation Council of India, Member, ex officio;

(h) Chairperson, National Trust for the Welfare of Persons with Autism, Cerebral Palsy, Mental Retardation and Multiple Disabilities, Member, ex officio;

(i)   Chairman-cum-Managing Director, National Handicapped Finance Development Corporation, Member, ex officio;

(j) Chairman-cum-Managing Director, Artificial Limbs Manufacturing Corporation, Member, ex officio;

(k) Chairman, Railway Board, Member, ex officio;

(l) Director-General, Employment and Training, Ministry of Labour and Employment, Member, ex officio;

(m) Director, National Council for Educational Research and Training, Member, ex officio;

(n) Chairperson, National Council of Teacher Education, Member, ex officio;

(o) Chairperson, University Grants Commission, Member, ex officio;

(p) Chairperson, Medical Council of India, Member, ex officio;

(q) Directors of the following Institutes: —

(i) National Institute for the Visually Handicapped, Dehradun;

(ii) National Institute for the Mentally Handicapped, Secundrabad;

(iii) Pandit Deen Dayal Upadhyay Institute for the Physically Handicapped, New Delhi;

(iv) Ali Yavar Jung National Institute for the Hearing Handicapped, Mumbai;

(v)   National Institute for the Orthopaedically Handicapped, Kolkata;

(vi) National Institute of Rehabilitation Training and Research, Cuttack;

(vii) National Institute for Empowerment of Persons with Multiple Disabilities, Chennai;

(viii) National Institute for Mental Health and Sciences, Bangalore;

(ix) Indian Sign Language Research and Training Centre, New Delhi, Members, ex officio;

(r) Members to be nominated by the Central Government, —

(i) five Members who are experts in the field of disability and rehabilitation;

(ii) ten Members, as far as practicable, being persons with disabilities, to represent non-Governmental Organisations concerned with disabilities or disabled persons organisations:

Provided that out of the ten Members nominated, at least, five Members shall be women and at least one person each shall be from the Scheduled Castes and the Scheduled Tribes;

(iii) up to three representatives of national level chambers of commerce and industry;

(s) Joint Secretary to the Government of India dealing with the subject of disability policy, Member-Secretary, ex officio.

61. (1) Save as otherwise provided under this Act, a Member of the Central Advisory Board nominated under clause (r) of sub-section (2) of section 60 shall hold office for a term of three years from the date of his nomination:

Provided that such a Member shall, notwithstanding the expiration of his term, continue to hold office until his successor enters upon his office.

(2) The Central Government may, if it thinks fit, remove any Member nominated under clause (r) of sub-section (2) of section 60, before the expiry of his term of office after giving him a reasonable opportunity of showing cause

against the same.

(3) A Member nominated under clause (r) of sub-section (2) of section 60 may at any time resign his office by writing under his hand addressed to the Central Government and the seat of the said Member shall thereupon becomes vacant.

(4) A casual vacancy in the Central Advisory Board shall be filled by a fresh nomination and the person nominated to fill the vacancy shall hold office only for the remainder of the term for which the Member in whose place he was so nominated.

(5) A Member nominated under sub-clause (i) or sub-clause (iii) of clause (r) of sub-section (2) of section 60 shall be eligible for renomination.

(6) The Members nominated under sub-clause (i) and sub-clause (ii) of clause (r) of sub-section (2) of section 60 shall receive such allowances as may be prescribed by the Central Government.

62. (1) No person shall be a Member of the Central Advisory Board, who —

(a) is, or at any time has been, adjudged insolvent or has suspended payment of his debts or has compounded with his creditors, or

(b) is of unsound mind and stands so declared by a competent court, or

(c) is, or has been, convicted of an offence which, in the opinion of the Central Government, involves moral turpitude, or

(d) is, or at any time has been, convicted of an offence under this Act, or

(e) has so abused his position in the opinion of the Central Government as a Member so as to render his continuance in the office is prejudicial interests of the general public.

(2) No order of removal shall be made by the Central Government under this section unless the Member concerned has been given a reasonable opportunity of showing cause against the same.

(3) Notwithstanding anything contained in sub-section (1) or sub-section (5) of section 61, a Member who has been removed under this section shall not be eligible for renomination as a Member.

63. If a Member of the Central Advisory Board becomes subject to any of the disqualifications specified in section 62, his seat shall become vacant.

64. The Central Advisory Board shall meet at least once in every six months and shall observe such rules of procedure in regard to the transaction of business at its meetings as may be prescribed.

65. (1) Subject to the provisions of this Act, the Central Advisory Board on disability shall be the national-level consultative and advisory body on disability matters, and shall facilitate the continuous evolution of a comprehensive policy for the empowerment of persons with disabilities and the full enjoyment of rights.

(2) In particular and without prejudice to the generality of the foregoing provisions, the Central Advisory Board on disability shall perform the following functions, namely: –

(a) advise the Central Government and the State Governments on policies, programmes, legislation and projects with respect to disability;

(b) develop a national policy to address issues concerning persons with disabilities;

(c) review and coordinate the activities of all Departments of the Government and other Governmental and non-

Governmental Organisations which are dealing with matters relating to persons with disabilities;

(d) take up the cause of persons with disabilities with the concerned authorities and the international organisations with a view to provide for schemes and projects for the persons with disabilities in the national plans;

(e) recommend steps to ensure accessibility, reasonable accommodation, nondiscrimination for persons with disabilities vis-à-vis information, services and the built environment and their participation in social life;

(f) monitor and evaluate the impact of laws, policies and programmes to achieve full participation of persons with disabilities; and

(g) such other functions as may be assigned from time to time by the Central Government.

66. (1) Every State Government shall, by notification, constitute a body to be known as the State Advisory Board on disability to exercise the powers conferred on, and to perform the function assigned to it, under this Act.

(2) The State Advisory Board shall consist of —

(a) the Minister in charge of the Department in the State Government dealing with disability matters, Chairperson, ex officio;

(b) the Minister of State or the Deputy Minister in charge of the Department in the State Government dealing with disability matters, if any, Vice-Chairperson, ex officio;

(c) secretaries to the State Government in charge of the Departments of Disability Affairs, School Education, Literacy and Higher Education, Women and Child Development, Finance, Personnel and Training, Health and Family Welfare, Rural Development,

Panchayati Raj, Industrial Policy and Promotion, Labour and Employment, Urban Development, Housing and Urban Poverty Alleviation, Science and Technology, Information Technology, Public Enterprises, Youth Affairs and Sports, Road Transport and any other Department, which the State Government considers necessary, Members, ex officio;

(d) three Members of the State Legislature of whom two shall be elected by the Legislative Assembly and one by the Legislative Council, if any, and where there is no Legislative Council, three Members shall be elected by the Legislative Assembly, Members, ex officio;

(e) Members to be nominated by the State Government: —

(i) five Members who are experts in the field of disability and rehabilitation;

(ii) five Members to be nominated by the State Government by rotation to represent the districts in such manner as may be prescribed:

Provided that no nomination under this sub-clause shall be made except on the recommendation of the district administration concerned;

(iii) ten persons as far as practicable, being persons with disabilities, to represent non Governmental Organisations or associations which are concerned with disabilities:

Provided that out of the ten persons nominated under this clause, at least, five shall be women and at least one person each shall be from the Scheduled Castes and the Scheduled Tribes;

(iv) not more than three representatives of the State Chamber of Commerce and Industry;

(f) officer not below the rank of Joint Secretary in the Department dealing with disability matters in the

State Government, Member-Secretary, ex officio.

67. (1) Save as otherwise provided under this Act, a Member of the State Advisory Board nominated under clause (e) of sub-section (2) of section 66, shall hold office for a term of three years from the date of his nomination:

Provided that such a Member shall, notwithstanding the expiration of his term, continue to hold office until his successor enters upon his office.

(2) The State Government may, if it thinks fit, remove any Member nominated under clause (e) of sub-section (2) of section 66, before the expiry of his term of office after giving him a reasonable opportunity of showing cause against the same.

(3) A Member nominated under clause (e) of sub-section (2) of section 66 may at any time resign his office by writing under his hand addressed to the State Government and the seat of the said Member shall thereupon become vacant.

(4) A casual vacancy in the State Advisory Board shall be filled by a fresh nomination and the person nominated to fill the vacancy shall hold office only for the remainder of the term for which the Member in whose place he was so nominated.

(5) A Member nominated under sub-clause (i) or sub-clause (iii) of clause (e) of sub-section (2) of section 66 shall be eligible for renomination.

(6) the Members nominated under sub-clause (i) and sub-clause (ii) of clause (e) of sub-section (2) of section 66 shall receive such allowances as may be prescribed by the State Government.

68. (1) No person shall be a Member of the State Advisory Board, who—

(a) is, or at any time has been, adjudged insolvent or has

suspended payment of his debts or has compounded with his creditors, or

(b) is of unsound mind and stands so declared by a competent court, or

(c) is, or has been, convicted of an offence which, in the opinion of the State Government, involves moral turpitude, or

(d) is, or at any time has been, convicted of an offence under this Act, or

(e) has so abused in the opinion of the State Government his position as a Member as to render his continuance in the State Advisory Board detrimental to the interests of the general public.

(2) No order of removal shall be made by the State Government under this section unless the Member concerned has been given a reasonable opportunity of showing cause against the same.

(3) Notwithstanding anything contained in sub-section (1) or sub-section (5) of section

67, a Member who has been removed under this section shall not be eligible for renomination as a Member.

69. If a Member of the State Advisory Board becomes subject to any of the disqualifications specified in section 68 his seat shall become vacant.

70. The State Advisory Board shall meet at least once in every six months and shall observe such rules or procedure in regard to the transaction of business at its meetings as may be prescribed by the State Government.

71. (1) Subject to the provisions of this Act, the State Advisory Board shall be the State-level consultative and advisory body on disability matters, and shall facilitate the continuous evolution of a comprehensive policy for the empowerment of persons with disabilities and the full enjoyment of rights.

(2) In particular and without prejudice to the generality of the foregoing provisions, the State Advisory Board on disability shall perform the following functions, namely: —

(a) advise the State Government on policies, programmes, legislation and projects with respect to disability;

(b) develop a State policy to address issues concerning persons with disabilities;

(c) review and coordinate the activities of all Departments of the State Government and other Governmental and non-Governmental Organisations in the State which are dealing with matters relating to persons with disabilities;

(d) take up the cause of persons with disabilities with the concerned authorities and the international organisations with a view to provide for schemes and projects for the persons with disabilities in the State plans;

(e) recommend steps to ensure accessibility, reasonable accommodation, nondiscrimination for persons with disabilities, services and the built environment and their participation in social life on an equal basis with others;

(f) monitor and evaluate the impact of laws, policies and programmes designed to achieve full participation of persons with disabilities; and

(g) such other functions as may be assigned from time to time by the State Government.

72. The State Government shall constitute District-level Committee on disability to perform such functions as may be prescribed by it.

73. No act or proceeding of the Central Advisory Board on disability, a State Advisory Board on disability, or a District-level Committee on disability shall be called in question on the ground merely of the existence of any vacancy in or any defect in the constitution of such Board or Committee, as the case may be.

CHAPTER XII

CHIEF COMMISSIONER AND STATE COMMISSIONER FOR PERSONS WITH DISABILITIESE

74. (1) The Central Government may, by notification, appoint a Chief Commissioner for Persons with Disabilities (hereinafter referred to as the "Chief Commissioner") for the purposes of this Act.

(2) The Central Government may, by notification appoint two Commissioners to assist the Chief Commissioner, of which one Commissioner shall be a persons with disability.

(3) A person shall not be qualified for appointment as the Chief Commissioner or Commissioner unless he has special knowledge or practical experience in respect of matters relating to rehabilitation.

(4) The salary and allowances payable to and other terms and conditions of service (including pension, gratuity and other retirement benefits) of the Chief Commissioner and Commissioners shall be such as may be prescribed by the Central Government.

(5) The Central Government shall determine the nature and categories of officers and other employees required to assist the Chief Commissioner in the discharge of his functions and provide the Chief Commissioner with such officers and other employees as it thinks fit.

(6) The officers and employees provided to the Chief Commissioner shall discharge their functions under the general superintendence and control of the Chief Commissioner.

(7) The salaries and allowances and other conditions of service of officers and employees shall be such as may be prescribed by the Central Government.

(8) The Chief Commissioner shall be assisted by an advisory committee comprising of not more than eleven members drawn from the experts from different disabilities in such manner as may be prescribed by the Central Government.

75. (1) The Chief Commissioner shall —

(a) identify, suo motu or otherwise, the provisions of any law or policy, programme and procedures, which are inconsistent with this Act and recommend necessary corrective steps;

(b) inquire, suo motu or otherwise, deprivation of rights of persons with disabilities and safeguards available to them in respect of matters for which the Central Government is the appropriate Government and take up the matter with appropriate authorities for corrective action;

(c) review the safeguards provided by or under this Act or any other law for the time being in force for the protection of rights of persons with disabilities and recommend measures for their effective implementation;

(d) review the factors that inhibit the enjoyment of rights of persons with disabilities and recommend appropriate remedial measures;

(e) study treaties and other international instruments on the rights of persons with disabilities and make recommendations for their effective implementation;

(f) undertake and promote research in the field of the rights of persons with disabilities;

(g) promote awareness of the rights of persons with disabilities and the safeguards available for their protection;

(h) monitor implementation of the provisions of this Act and schemes, programmes meant for persons with disabilities;

(i) monitor utilisation of funds disbursed by the Central Government for the benefit of persons with disabilities; and

(j) perform such other functions as the Central Government may assign.

(2) The Chief Commissioner shall consult the Commissioners on any matter while discharging its functions under this Act.

76. Whenever the Chief Commissioner makes a recommendation to an authority in pursuance of clause (b) of section 75, that authority shall take necessary action on it, and inform the Chief Commissioner of the action taken within three months from the date of receipt of the recommendation:

Provided that where an authority does not accept a recommendation, it shall convey reasons for non-acceptance to the Chief Commissioner within a period of three months, and shall also inform the aggrieved person.

77. (1) The Chief Commissioner shall, for the purpose of discharging his functions under this Act, have the same powers of a civil court as are vested in a court under the Code of Civil Procedure, 1908 while trying a suit, in respect of the following matters, namely: —

(a) summoning and enforcing the attendance of witnesses;

(b) requiring the discovery and production of any documents;

(c) requisitioning any public record or copy thereof from any court or office;

(d) receiving evidence on affidavits; and

(e) issuing commissions for the examination of witnesses or documents.

(2) Every proceeding before the Chief Commissioner shall be a judicial proceeding within the meaning of sections 193 and 228 of the Indian Penal Code and the Chief Commissioner shall be deemed to be a civil court for the purposes of section 195 and Chapter XXVI of the Code of Criminal Procedure, 1973.

78. (1) The Chief Commissioner shall submit an annual report to the Central Government and may at any time submit special reports on any matter, which, in his opinion, is of such urgency or importance that it shall not be deferred till submission of the annual report.

(2) The Central Government shall cause the annual and the special reports of the Chief Commissioner to be laid before each House of Parliament, along with a memorandum of action taken or proposed to be taken on his recommendations and the reasons for non acceptance the recommendations, if any.

(3) The annual and special reports shall be prepared in such form, manner and contain such details as may be prescribed by the Central Government.

79. (1) The State Government may, by notification, appoint a State Commissioner for Persons with Disabilities (hereinafter referred to as the "State Commissioner") for the purposes of this Act.

(2) A person shall not be qualified for appointment as the State Commissioner unless he has special knowledge or practical experience in respect of matters relating to rehabilitation.

(3) The salary and allowances payable to and other terms and conditions of service (including pension, gratuity and other retirement benefits) of the State Commissioner shall be such as may be prescribed by the State Government.

(4) The State Government shall determine the nature and categories of officers and other employees required to assist the State Commissioner in the discharge of his functions and provide the State Commissioner with such officers and other employees as it thinks fit.

(5) The officers and employees provided to the State Commissioner shall discharge his functions under the general superintendence and control of the State Commissioner.

(6) The salaries and allowances and other conditions of service of officers and employees shall be such as may be prescribed by the State Government.

(7) The State Commissioner shall be assisted by an advisory committee comprising of not more than five members drawn from the experts in the disability sector in such manner as may be prescribed by the State Government.

80. The State Commissioner shall—

(a) identify, suo motu or otherwise, provision of any law or policy, programme and procedures, which are in consistent with this Act, and recommend necessary corrective steps;

(b) inquire, suo motu or otherwise deprivation of rights of persons with disabilities and safeguards available to them in respect of matters for which the State

Government is the appropriate Government and take up the matter with appropriate authorities for corrective action;

(c) review the safeguards provided by or under this Act or any other law for the time being in force for the protection of rights of persons with disabilities and recommend measures for their effective implementation;

(d) review the factors that inhibit the enjoyment of rights of persons with disabilities and recommend appropriate remedial measures;

(e) undertake and promote research in the field of the rights of persons with disabilities;

(f) promote awareness of the rights of persons with disabilities and the safeguards available for their protection;

(g) monitor implementation of the provisions of this Act and schemes, programmes meant for persons with disabilities;

(h) monitor utilisation of funds disbursed by the State Government for the benefits of persons with disabilities; and

(i) perform such other functions as the State Government may assign.

81. Whenever the State Commissioner makes a recommendation to an authority in pursuance of clause (b) of section 80, that authority shall take necessary action on it, and inform the State Commissioner of the action taken within three months from the date of receipt of the recommendation:

Provided that where an authority does not accept a recommendation, it shall convey reasons for non-acceptance to the State Commissioner for Persons with

Disabilities within the period of three months, and shall also inform the aggrieved person.

82. (1) The State Commissioner shall, for the purpose of discharging their functions under this Act, have the same powers of a civil court as are vested in a court under the Code of Civil Procedure, 1908 while trying a suit, in respect of the following matters, namely: —

(a) summoning and enforcing the attendance of witnesses;

(b) requiring the discovery and production of any documents;

(c) requisitioning any public record or copy thereof from any court or office;

(d) receiving evidence on affidavits; and

(e) issuing commissions for the examination of witnesses or documents.

(2) Every proceeding before the State Commissioner shall be a judicial proceeding within the meaning of sections 193 and 228 of the Indian Penal Code and the State Commissioners shall be deemed to be a civil court for the purposes of section 195 and Chapter XXVI of the Code of Criminal Procedure, 1973.

83. (1) The State Commissioner shall submit an annual report to the State Government and may at any time submit special reports on any matter, which, in its opinion, is of such urgency or importance that it shall not be deferred till submission of the annual report.

(2) The State Government shall cause the annual and the special reports of the State Commissioner for persons with disabilities to be laid before each House of State Legislature where it consists of two Houses or where such Legislature consist of one House, before that House along with a memorandum of action taken or proposed to be taken on the recommendation of the State Commissioner

and the reasons for non-acceptance the recommendations, if any.

(3) The annual and special reports shall be prepared in such form, manner and contain such details as may be prescribed by the State Government.

CHAPTER XIII

SPECIAL COURT

84. For the purpose of providing speedy trial, the State Government shall, with the concurrence of the Chief Justice of the High Court, by notification, specify for each district, a Court of Session to be a Special Court to try the offences under this Act.

85. (1) For every Special Court, the State Government may, by notification, specify a Public Prosecutor or appoint an advocate, who has been in practice as an advocate for not less than seven years, as a Special Public Prosecutor for the purpose of conducting cases in that Court.

(2) The Special Public Prosecutor appointed under sub-section (1) shall be entitled to receive such fees or remuneration as may be prescribed by the State Government.

CHAPTER XIV

NATIONAL FUND FOR PERSONS WITH DISABILITIES

86. (1) There shall be constituted a Fund to be called the National Fund for persons with disabilities and there shall be credited thereto —

(a) all sums available under the Fund for people with disabilities, constituted vide notification No. S.O.

573 (E), dated the 11th August, 1983 and the Trust Fund for Empowerment of Persons with Disabilities, constituted vide notification No. 30-03/2004-DDII, dated the 21st November, 2006, under the Charitable Endowment Act, 1890.

(b) all sums payable by banks, corporations, financial institutions in pursuance of judgment dated the 16th April, 2004 of the Hon'ble Supreme Court in Civil Appeal Nos. 4655 and 5218 of 2000;

(c) all sums received by way of grant, gifts, donations, benefactions, bequests or transfers;

(d) all sums received from the Central Government including grants-in-aid;

(e) all sums from such other sources as may be decided by the Central Government.

(2) The Fund for persons with disabilities shall be utilised and managed in such manner as may be prescribed.

87. (1) The Central Government shall maintain proper accounts and other relevant records and prepare an annual statement of accounts of the Fund including the income and expenditure accounts in such form as may be prescribed in consultation with the Comptroller and Auditor-General of India.

(2) The accounts of the Fund shall be audited by the Comptroller and Auditor-General of India at such intervals as may be specified by him and any expenditure incurred by him in connection with such audit shall be payable from the Fund to the Comptroller and Auditor-General of India.

(3) The Comptroller and Auditor-General of India and any other person appointed by him in connection with the audit of the accounts of the Fund shall have the same rights, privileges and authority in connection with

such audit as the Comptroller and Auditor- General of India generally has in connection with the audit of the Government accounts, and in particular, shall have the right to demand production of books of account, connected vouchers and other documents and papers and to inspect any of the offices of the Fund.

(4) The accounts of the Fund as certified by the Comptroller and Auditor-General of India or any other person appointed by him in this behalf, together with the audit report thereon, shall be laid before each House of Parliament by the Central Government.

CHAPTER XV

STATE FUND FOR PERSONS WITH DISABILITIES

88. (1) There shall be constituted a Fund to be called the State Fund for persons with disabilities by a State Government in such manner as may be prescribed by the State Government.

(2) The State Fund for persons with disabilities shall be utilised and managed in such manner as may be prescribed by the State Government.

(3) Every State Government shall maintain proper accounts and other relevant records of the State Fund for persons with disabilities including the income and expenditure accounts in such form as may be prescribed by the State Government in consultation with the Comptroller and Auditor-General of India.

(4) The accounts of the State Fund for persons with disabilities shall be audited by the Comptroller and Auditor-General of India at such intervals as may be specified by him and any expenditure incurred by him in connection with such audit shall be payable from the State

Fund to the Comptroller and Auditor-General of India.

(5) The Comptroller and Auditor-General of India and any person appointed by him in connection with the audit of the accounts of the State Fund for persons with disabilities shall have the same rights, privileges and authority in connection with such audit as the Comptroller and Auditor-General of India generally has in connection with the audit of the Government accounts, and in particular, shall have right to demand production of books of accounts, connected vouchers and other documents and papers and to inspect any of the offices of the State Fund.

(6) The accounts of the State Fund for persons with disabilites as certified by the Comptroller and Auditor-General of India or any other person appointed by him in this behalf together with the audit report thereon shall be laid before each House of the State Legislature where it consists of two Houses or where such Legislature consists of one House before that House.

CHAPTER XVI

OFFENCES AND PENALTIES

89. Any person who contravenes any of the provisions of this Act, or of any rule made thereunder shall for first contravention be punishable with fine which may extend to ten thousand rupees and for any subsequent contravention with fine which shall not be less than fifty thousand rupees but which may extend to five lakh rupees.

90. (1) Where an offence under this Act has been committed by a company, every person who at the time the offence was committed, was in charge of, and was responsible to, the company for the conduct of the business of the company, as well as the company, shall be deemed to be

guilty of the offence and shall be liable to be proceeded against and punished accordingly:

Provided that nothing contained in this sub-section shall render any such person liable to any punishment provided in this Act, if he proves that the offence was committed without his knowledge or that he had exercised all due diligence to prevent the commission of such offence.

(2) Notwithstanding anything contained in sub-section (1), where an offence under this Act has been committed by a company and it is proved that the offence has been committed with the consent or connivance of, or is attributable to any neglect on the part of any director, manager, secretary or other officer of the company, such director, manager, secretary or other officer shall also be deemed to be guilty of that offence and shall be liable to be proceeded against and punished accordingly.

Explanation. — For the purposes of this section, —

(a) "company" means any body corporate and includes a firm or other association of individuals; and

(b) "director", in relation to a firm, means a partner in the firm.

91. Whoever, fraudulently avails or attempts to avail any benefit meant for persons with benchmark disabilities, shall be punishable with imprisonment for a term which may extend to two years or with fine which may extend to one lakh rupees or with both.

92. Whoever, —

(a) intentionally insults or intimidates with intent to humiliate a person with disability in any place within public view;

(b) assaults or uses force to any person with disability with intent to dishonor him or outrage the modesty of a woman with disability;

(c) having the actual charge or control over a person with disability voluntarily or knowingly denies food or fluids to him or her;

(d) being in a position to dominate the will of a child or woman with disability and uses that position to exploit her sexually;

(e) voluntarily injures, damages or interferes with the use of any limb or sense or any supporting device of a person with disability;

(f) performs, conducts or directs any medical procedure to be performed on a woman with disability which leads to or is likely to lead to termination of pregnancy without her express consent except in cases where medical procedure for termination of pregnancy is done in severe cases of disability and with the opinion of a registered medical practitioner and also with the consent of the guardian of the woman with disability, shall be punishable with imprisonment for a term which shall not be less than six months but which may extend to five years and with fine.

93. Whoever, fails to produce any book, account or other documents or to furnish any statement, information or particulars which, under this Act or any order, or direction made or given there under, is duty bound to produce or furnish or to answer any question put in pursuance of the provisions of this Act or of any order, or direction made or given thereunder, shall be punishable with fine which may extend to twenty-five thousand rupees in respect of each offence, and in case of continued failure or refusal, with further fine which may extend to one thousand rupees for each day, of continued failure or refusal after the date of original order imposing punishment of fine.

94. No Court shall take cognizance of an offence alleged to have been committed by an employee of the appropriate

Government under this Chapter, except with the previous sanction of the appropriate Government or a complaint is filed by an officer authorised by it in this behalf.

95. Where an act or omission constitutes an offence punishable under this Act and also under any other Central or State Act, then, notwithstanding anything contained in any other law for the time being in force, the offender found guilty of such offence shall be liable to punishment only under such Act as provides for punishment which is greater in degree.

CHAPTER XVII

MISCELLANEOUS

96. The provisions of this Act shall be in addition to, and not in derogation of, the provisions of any other law for the time being in force.

97. No suit, prosecution or other legal proceeding shall lie against the appropriate Government or any officer of the appropriate Government or any officer or employee of the Chief Commissioner or the State Commissioner for anything which is in good faith done or intended to be done under this Act or the rules made thereunder.

98. (1) If any difficulty arises in giving effect to the provisions of this Act, the Central Government may, by order, published in the Official Gazette, make such provisions or give such directions, not inconsistent with the provisions of this Act, as may appear to it to be necessary or expedient for removing the difficulty:

Provided that no such order shall be made under this section after the expiry of the period of two years from the date of commencement of this Act.

(2) Every order made under this section shall be laid as

soon as may be, after it is made, before each House of Parliament.

99. (1) On the recommendations made by the appropriate Government or otherwise, if the Central Government is satisfied that it is necessary or expedient so to do, it may, by notification, amend the Schedule and any such notification being issued, the Schedule shall be deemed to have been amended accordingly.

(2) Every such notification shall, as soon as possible after it is issued, shall be laid before each House of Parliament.

100. (1) The Central Government may, subject to the condition of previous publication, by notification, make rules for carrying out the provisions of this Act.

(2) In particular, and without prejudice to the generality of the foregoing power, such rules may provide for all or any of the following matters, namely: —

(a) the manner of constituting the Committee for Research on Disability under sub-section (2) of section 6;

(b) the manner of notifying the equal opportunity policy under sub-section (1) of section 21;

(c) the form and manner of maintaining records by every establishment under sub-section (1) of section 22;

(d) the manner of maintenance of register of complaints by grievance redressal officer under sub-section (3) of section 23;

(e) the manner of furnishing information and return by establishment to the Special Employment Exchange under section 36;

(f) the composition of the Assessment Board under sub-section (2) and manner of assessment to be made by the Assessment Board under sub-section (3) of section 38;

(g) rules for person with disabilites laying down the standards of accessibility under section 40;

(h) the manner of application for issuance of certificate of disability under sub-section (1) and form of certificate of disability under sub-section (2) of section 58;

(i) the allowances to be paid to nominated Members of the Central Advisory Board under sub-section (6) of section 61;

(j) the rules of procedure for transaction of business in the meetings of the Central Advisory Board under section 64;

(k) the salaries and allowances and other conditions of services of Chief Commissioner and Commissioners under sub-section (4) of section 74;

(l) the salaries and allowances and conditions of services of officers and staff of the Chief Commissioner under sub-section (7) of section 74;

(m) the composition and manner of appointment of experts in the advisory committee under sub-section (8) of section 74;

(n) the form, manner and content of annual report to be prepared and submitted by the Chief Commissioner under sub-section (3) of section 78;

(o) the procedure, manner of utilisation and management of the Fund under sub-section (2) of section 86; and

(p) the form for preparation of accounts of Fund under sub-section (1) of section 87.

(3) Every rule made under this Act shall be laid, as soon as may be after it is made, before each House of Parliament while it is in session, for a total period of thirty days which may be comprised in one session or in two or more successive sessions, and if, before the expiry of the session

immediately following the session or the successive sessions aforesaid, both Houses agree in making any modification in the rule or both Houses agree that the rule should not be made, the rule shall thereafter have effect only in such modified form or be of no effect, as the case may be; so, however, that any such modification or annulment shall be without prejudice to the validity of anything previously done under that rule.

101. (1) The State Government may, subject to the condition of previous publication, by notification, make rules for carrying out the provisions of this Act, not later than six months from the date of commencement of this Act.

(2) In particular, and without prejudice to the generality of foregoing powers, such rules may provide for all or any of the following matters, namely: —

(a) the manner of constituting the Committee for Research on Disablity under sub-section (2) of section 5;

(b) the manner of providing support of a limited guardian under sub-section (1) of section 14;

(c) the form and manner of making an application for certificate of registration under sub-section (1) of section 51;

(d) the facilities to be provided and standards to be met by institutions for grant of certificate of registration under sub-section (3) of section 51;

(e) the validity of certificate of registration, the form of, and conditions attached to, certificate of registration under sub-section (4) of section 51;

(f) the period of disposal of application for certificate of registration under sub-section (7) of section 51;

(g) the period within which an appeal to be made under sub-section (1) of section 53;

(h) the time and manner of appealing against the order of certifying authority under sub-section (1) and manner of disposal of such appeal under sub-section (2) of section 59;

(i) the allowances to be paid to nominated Members of the State Advisory Board under sub-section (6) of section 67;

(j) the rules of procedure for transaction of business in the meetings of the State Advisory Board under section 70;

(k) the composition and functions of District Level Committee under section 72;

(l) salaries, allowances and other conditions of services of the State Commissioner under sub-section (3) of section 79;

(m) the salaries, allowances and conditions of services of officers and staff of the State Commissioner under sub-section (3) of section 79;

(n) the composition and manner of appointment of experts in the advisory committee under sub-section (7) of section 79;

(o) the form, manner and content of annual and special reports to be prepared and submitted by the State Commissioner under sub-section (3) of section 83;

(p) the fee or remuneration to be paid to the Special Public Prosecutor under sub-section (2) of section 85;

(q) the manner of constitution of State Fund for persons with disabilities under sub-section (1), and the manner of utilisation and management of State Fund under sub-section (2) of section 88;

(r) the form for preparation of accounts of the State Fund for persons with disabilities under sub-section (3) of section 88.

(3) Every rule made by the State Government under this Act shall be laid, as soon as may be after it is made, before each House of the State Legislature where it consists of two Houses, or where such State Legislature consists of one House, before that House.

102. (1) The Persons with Disabilities (Equal Opportunity Protection of Rights and Full Participation) Act, 1995 is hereby repealed.

(2) Notwithstanding the repeal of the said Act, anything done or any action taken under the said Act, shall be deemed to have been done or taken under the corresponding provisions of this Act.

THE SCHEDULE

[*See* clause (zc) of section 2]

SPECIFIED DISABILITY

1. Physical disability.—

A. Locomotor disability (a person's inability to execute distinctive activities associated with movement of self and objects resulting from affliction of musculoskeletal or nervous system or both), including—

    (a) "leprosy cured person" means a person who has been cured of leprosy but is suffering from—

    (i) loss of sensation in hands or feet as well as loss of sensation and paresis in the eye and eye-lid but with no manifest deformity;

    (ii) manifest deformity and paresis but having sufficient mobility in their hands and feet to enable them to engage in normal economic activity;

(iii) extreme physical deformity as well as advanced age which prevents him/her from undertaking any gainful occupation, and the expression "leprosy cured" shall construed accordingly;

(b) "cerebral palsy" means a Group of non-progressive neurological condition affecting body movements and muscle coordination, caused by damage to one or more specific areas of the brain, usually occurring before, during or shortly after birth;

(c) "dwarfism" means a medical or genetic condition resulting in an adult height of 4 feet 10 inches (147 centimeters) or less;

(d) "muscular dystrophy" means a group of hereditary genetic muscle disease that weakens the muscles that move the human body and persons with multiple dystrophy have incorrect and missing information in their genes, which prevents them from making the proteins they need for healthy muscles. It is characterised by progressive skeletal muscle weakness, defects in muscle proteins, and the death of muscle cells and tissue;

(e) "acid attack victims" means a person disfigured due to violent assaults by throwing of acid or similar corrosive substance.

B. Visual impairment —

(a) "blindness" means a condition where a person has any of the following conditions, after best correction —

(i)   total absence of sight; or

(ii) visual acuity less than 3/60 or less than 10/200 (Snellen) in the better eye with best possible correction; or

(iii) limitation of the field of vision subtending an angle of less than 10 degree.

(b) "low-vision" means a condition where a person has any of the following conditons, namely: —

(i) visual acuity not exceeding 6/18 or less than 20/60 upto 3/60 or upto 10/200 (Snellen) in the better eye with best possible corrections; or

(ii) limitation of the field of vision subtending an angle of less than 40 degree up to 10 degree.

C. Hearing impairment—

   (a)   "deaf" means persons having 70 DB hearing loss in speech frequencies in both ears;

   (b)   "hard of hearing" means person having 60 DB to 70 DB hearing loss in speech frequencies in both ears;

D. "speech and language disability" means a permanent disability arising out of conditions such as laryngectomy or aphasia affecting one or more components of speech and language due to organic or neurological causes.

2.   Intellectual disability, a condition characterised by significant limitation both in intellectual functioning (rasoning, learning, problem solving) and in adaptive behaviour which covers a range of every day, social and practical skills, including—

(a) "specific learning disabilities" means a heterogeneous group of conditions wherein there is a deficit in processing language, spoken or written, that may manifest itself as a difficulty to comprehend, speak, read, write, spell, or to do mathematical calculations and includes such conditions as perceptual disabilities, dyslexia, dysgraphia, dyscalculia, dyspraxia and developmental aphasia;

(b) "autism spectrum disorder" means a neuro-developmental condition typically appearing in the first three years of life that significantly affects a person's ability to communicate, understand relationships and relate to others, and is frequently associated with unusal or stereotypical rituals or behaviours.

3. Mental behaviour, —

"mental illness" means a substantial disorder of thinking, mood, perception, orientation or memory that grossly impairs judgment, behaviour, capacity to recognize reality or ability to meet the ordinary demands of life, but does not include retardation which is a condition of arrested or incomplete development of mind of a person, specially characterised by subnormality of intelligence.

4. Disability caused due to —

(a)   chronic neurological conditions, such as —

(i)   "multiple sclerosis" means an inflammatory, nervous system disease in which the myelin sheaths around the axons of nerve cells of the brain and spinal cord are damaged, leading to demyelination and affecting the ability of nerve cells in the brain and spinal cord to communicate with each other;

(ii) "parkinson's disease" means a progressive disease of the nervous system marked by tremor, muscular rigidity, and slow, imprecise movement, chiefly affecting middle-aged and elderly people associated with degeneration of the basal ganglia of the brain and a deficiency of the neurotransmitter dopamine.

(b)   Blood disorder —

(i)   "haemophilia" means an inheritable disease, usually affecting only male but transmitted by women to their male children, characterised by loss or impairment of the normal clotting ability of blood so that a minor would may result in fatal bleeding;

(ii) "thalassemia" means a group of inherited disorders

characterised by reduced or absent amounts of haemoglobin.

(iii) "sickle cell disease" means a hemolytic disorder characterised by chronic anemia, painful events, and various complications due to associated tissue and organ damage; "hemolytic" refers to the destruction of the cell membrane of red blood cells resulting in the release of hemoglobin.

5. Multiple Disabilities (more than one of the above specified disabilities) including deaf blindness which means a condition in which a person may have combination of hearing and visual impairments causing severe communication, developmental, and educational problems.

6. Any other category as may be notified by the Central Government.

LIST OF EXPERTS INTERVIEWED

State Commissioner for Persons with Disabilities Act, Sheshadripuram, Bangalore

- Mr. V.S. Basavaraju (2019), Personal Interview, State Commissioner for Persons with Disabilities Act, Sheshadripuram, Bangalore

District Commissioner's Office:

- Mr. Amarnath K.M.(2018), Personal Interview, District Disable's Welfare Officer, Dharwad

Siddharoodmath, Hubballi

- Mr. Annappa Koli (2018), Personal Interview, Senior Teacher, Government residential school for blind boys, Siddharoodmath, Hubballi

    Shri Aarooda Education Society's Residential School for Blind, Hubballi

- Mrs. Vidyavathi Bakale (2018) Personal Interview, Head Mastress, Shri Aarooda Education Society's Residential School for Blind, Hubballi

J.S.S. Educational Institutions

- Smt. Sadhana S.(2018), Personal Interview, Principal, Personal Interview, J.S.S. Shri Manjunatheshwara Central School, Dharwad

- Smt. Bharathi V. Shanbagh (2018), Personal Interview, Principal, J.S.S. R.S. Hukkerikar Arts, Commerce and Science Pre-University College, Vidyagiri Dharwad

- Mr. G. Krishnamurthy (2018), Personal Interview, Principal, J.S.S. Banashankari Arts, Commerce and S.K. Gubbi Science Degree College, Dharwad

Mr. D.G. Shetty Educational Institutions

- Mr. D.G. Shetty (2018), Personal Interview, President of D.G. Shetty Educational Society and is also the Principal to the society's running Pre-university, Degree courses in the field of arts, science and commerce stream and Masters in commerce post-graduation courses

IGNOU, Dharwad

- Mr. Suraj Jain (2018), Personal Interview, Coordinator for IGNOU, Dharwad

  Chikenkoppad Shree Chennaveer Sharanara's Welfare Ashram for Blind, Hubballi

- Mr. Shankarayya V. Hiremath (2018), Personal Interview, Manager, Chikenkoppad Shree Chennaveer Sharanara's Welfare Ashram for Blind, Hubballi

Samarthanam trust for the Disabled, Dharwad

- Revansiddayya G. S.(2018), Personal Interview, Regional Manager for Dharwad Division and as North Karnataka Head in terms of co-ordination for any events in these regions

Sahana Charitable Trust for the Disabled, Dharwad

- Mr. Ramachander Dhongade(2018), Personal Interview, Co-ordinator, North Karnataka Braille Library and Citizen's Reading Room, Sahana Charitable Trust for the Disabled, Dharwad

Samadrishti Kshamata Vikas Evam Anusandhan Mandal (SAKSHAM)

- Mr. S. B. Shetty(2018), Personal Interview,President, SAKSHAM, Hubballi

- Dr. Vittal S. Managoli(2018), Personal Interview, Vice President North Karnataka Region, SAKSHAM, Dharwad

- Mr. Girish Joshi(2018), Personal Interview, Chief Secretary, SAKSHAM, Hubballi

National Association for the Blind, Karnataka branch, Bangalore

- M. Srinivas, (2018) Personal Interview, Chief Executive Officer, National Association for the Blind (NAB), Karnataka branch, Bangalore

- D. GopalKrishna (2018), Project Manager, National Association for the Blind (NAB), Karnataka branch, Bangalore

National Federation of the Blind, Bangalore

- Mr Hemanth Umar D. (2018), Manager, National Federation of the Blind, Bangalore

Financial Institutions

- Mr N. S. Parvatiar(2018), Personal Interview, Chief Manager, Law Department, SBI, Hubballi

- Mr Vihwanath Hegde (2018), Personal Interview, Chief Manager (Human Reource), SBI, Hubballi

- Mr Vinay R. (2018), Personal Interview, Deputy Manager, ICICI Hubballi Branch, Hubballi

Karnataka Institute of Medical Science

- Dr. Sunil Gokhale (2018), Personal Interview, Lecturer in Community Medicine, KIMS, Hubballi

- Dr. Rajashelar Dyaberi (2018), Personal Interview, Deputy Medical Superintendent, Assistant Professor in Opthomology, KIMS, Hubballi

District Employment Exchange, Hubballi

- Mrs. Sadhana Pote (IAS) (2018), Personal Interview,

Asst. Director for District Employment Exchange Office, Navanagar, Hubballi

APPENDIX 4

List of Tables

Table No.	Title	Page
1	Source: Office of the Registrar General & Census Commissioner, India; GOI	2
2	Source: Government of Karnataka, Handbook of Karnataka Schemes,2016	38
3	Categories of visual disability as updated by KIMS	52
4	Governmental and Non-Governmental Institutions in Hubballi-Dharwad	53
5	Staffs in Blind Boys Government Residential School, Hubballi	54
6	No. of persons with disabilities registered for the Under Graduate and Post Graduate Courses in the affiliated colleges	91
7	No. of persons with disabilities registered in Dharwad University Campus	91

List of Figures

Table No.	Title	Page
20	Dr. D.G. Shetty Educational Society, Dharwad	96
21	J.S.S Shri Manjunatheshwara Central School, Dharwad	97
22	J.S.S. R.S. Hukkerikar Arts, Commerce and Science Pre-University College, Vidyagiri Dharwad	97

APPENDIX 5

LIST OF STATUTES AND CONVENTIONS

- Mental Health Care Act, 2017
- The Constitution of India
- The National Trust for Welfare of Persons with Autism, Cerebral Palsy, Mental Retardation and Multiple Disabilities Act, 1999
- The Persons with Disabilities (Equal Opportunities, Protection of Rights and Full Participation Act, 1995
- The Rehabilitation Council of India Act, 1992
- The Rights of Persons with Disabilities Act, 2016
- The United Nations Convention on the Rights of Persons with Disabilities

APPENDIX 6

REFERENCES

Ali, Baquer and Anjali Sharma (1997), *Disability: Challenges Vs Responses*, (New Delhi: Concerned Action Now, 1997).

*Beijing Declaration adopted on 12 March 2000 at the World NGO Summit on Disability. Beijing, People's Republic of China, [Online: web] Assessed 12 May 2018

URL: http://www.rehab-international.org/aboutri/ beijingdeclaration.html

*Convention on the Rights of Persons with Disabilities (CRPD), Dec. 6, 2006, [Online: web] Assessed 12 May 2018 URL: http://www.un.org/disabilities/convention/ conventionfull.shtml

*CRPD Committee (2016). General Comment No 4 Article 24: Right to Inclusive Education, [Online: web] Accessed 11 February 2018

URL: http://www.ohchr.org/EN/HRBodies/CRPD/Pages/ GC.aspx

Deborah, Stienstra et. al. (2002), "Base line Assessment: Inclusion and Disability in World Bank Activities, Canadian Centre on Disability Studies", [Online: web] Assessed 12 May 2018

URL:http://www.iddc.org.uk/dis_dev/mainstreaming/ incl_dis_wildbank.doc

Disability Rights Activists say Jaitley's budget a 'big disappointment', *Indian Express*, New Delhi, September 28,

2018.

*ESCAP, *Economic and Social Survey of Asia and the Pacific*, United Nations Publication, Sales No.E.03.II.F.11, 2003.

Elwan, Ann (1999), "Poverty and Disability: A Survey of the Literature Social Protection Discussion Paper No.9932, The World Bank Group", [Online: web] Accessed 14th January 2019

URL:http://siteresources.worldbank.org/DISABILITY/Resources/2806581172608138489/PovertyDisabElwan.pdf

Esme Grant and Rhonda Neuhaus, Liberty and Justice for All: The Convention on the Rights of Persons with Disabilities, *19 ILSA J. Int'l and Comp. L. 347 (2013)*

European Year of Disabled Persons (2003), [Online: web] Accessed 15th January 2019

URL://http://www.edf-feph.org/en/events/year/year.htm

*G-8 Summit to Inclusion (2002), [Online: web] Accessed 15th January 2019

URL:http://www.g7.utoronto.ca/evaluations/2002kananaskis/assessment_africaplan.html

*Government of India, Ministry of Urban Development, Service Level Benchmark, Urban Transport, http://www.utbenchmark.in (last updated Dec.7, 2018)

Hubballi and Dharwad City Census 2011 [Online: web] Accessed 15th September 2018 URL: data see http://www.census2011.co.in

Habibi, Gulbadan (1999), "UNICEF and Children with Disabilities", *Education Update*, 2(4):7-33.

Jha, Martand The history of India's Disability Rights Movement, The Dipomat, December 21. 2016

K.C. Deepika, Karnataka Budget: Survey of Persons with Disabilities announced, *The Hindu*, 6 July, 2018.

Keller, Helen (2009), *Story of My Life*, Cosimo, Inc.,

*Kochi Declaration (2003), Kochi, Kerala, India; available at http://www.inclusion-international.org/site_uploads/1119008867197086195.pdf

Koppa, Nijaguni Dhindala, Blind's educational life lightened by Braille system, *Vijaya Karnataka Newspaper*, 30th June, 2018, Hubballi.

Lang, Raymond (2006), "Human Rights and Disability-New and Dynamic Perspective with the United Nations Convention on Disability", *Asian and Pacific Disability Rehabilitation* Journal, 17(1):3-11.

Limaye, Sandhya "Social Empowerment for differently abled", *Yojana* , August 2018

Moore and Slee,   R. Disability Studies, Education and Exclusion in N. Watson, A. Roulstone and C. Thomas (eds) *Handbook of Disability Studies,* (London: Routledge, 2012) 225-239

Mishra, Prabhati Nayak, Proper Implementation of Rights of Persons with Disabilities Act, 2016: SC grants three months' time for States and UTs, *www.livelaw.in* January 28, 2018

National Federation of Blind Souvenir (2018), Karnataka: NFB.

*National Human Rights Commission, Annual Report 2004—2005 of National Human Rights Commission , New Delhi.

*National Human Rights Commission (2010), Know your Rights, Rights of Persons with Disabilities, Know Your Rights Series, New Delhi.

*National Policy of Persons with Disabilities, Ministry of Social Justice and Empowerment, New Delhi.

Peters, Susan J (2003), "Inclusive education: Achieving education for all by including those with Disabilities and Special education needs", [Online: web] Accessed 6

September 2018

URL:http://siteresources.worldbank.org/DISABILITY/
Resources/280658-1172610312075/InclusiveEduPeters.pdf

Prakash, Jayanti (2005), "Inclusive education: voices from the other side". *I.J.D.S*, 1(1):92-113.

Quinn, Gerard (2009), A Short Guide to the United Nations Convention on the Rights of Persons with Disabilities, 1 *Eur. Y.B. Disability L, 89*

T. Degener and Y Koster-Dreese (ed.) (1995), *Human Rights and Disabled Persons*, Dordrech; Boston :Nijhoff.

Lang, Raymond (2006), "Human Rights and Disability-New and Dynamic Perspective with the United Nations Convention on Disability", *Asian and Pacific Disability Rehabilitation Journal*, 17(1):3-11.

*UNESCO (2002), World Education Forum Final Report, Part II: Improving the quality and equity of education for all. Sub section entitled "Meeting special and diverse education needs: making inclusive education a reality"

*UNESCO (2005), Guidelines for Inclusion: Ensuring Access to Education for All. [Online: web] Accessed 6 September 2018

http://unesdoc.unesco.org/images/0014/001402/140224e.
pdf

*United Nations (1994), *United Nations in the field of Human Rights*, New York.

Verma, Ramesh, Pardeep Khanna et., al,(2011) "The National Programme for Control of Blindness in India", *The Australasian Medical Journal;* 4(1): 1-3

Yadava, Shalini (2013) "Inclusive Education: Challenges and Prospects in India", *Educationia Confab*, Vol.2, No.4

www.ingramcontent.com/pod-product-compliance
Lightning Source LLC
LaVergne TN
LVHW041508170726

843492LV00005B/1405